T0134047

IoT Benefits and Growth Opportunities for the Telecom Industry

This critical and forward-looking book features a case study of Bell Canada Enterprises (BCE) Inc., which highlights IoT-based business models in the industry. The study reveals that telecom operators have started implementing IoT projects. However, true revenue streams are yet to materialize. Ten IoT-based business models have been identified at BCE Inc. The book points out that operators do leverage existing infrastructure in terms of broadband fiber and mobile connectivity in part, and resort to partnerships and acquisitions to acquire much-needed knowledge, technology, and smart devices.

Regarding the effect of IoT on the telecoms' revenue streams, the book reveals how new entrants, who are not necessarily in the telecom industry, have impacted the old players' revenue streams. Over-the-Top (OTT) services like YouTube, WhatsApp, IPTV, and Netflix are the biggest culprits. Seven key technological drivers for IoT are identified and include widespread wireless connectivity; the availability and affordability of microcontrollers; sensors and actuators; the decreasing cost of bandwidth; the recent implementation of IPv6, and the ongoing development of 5G network, as well as the use of cloud computing and analytics.

Finally, the PESTLE (political, economic, socio-cultural, technological, legal, and environmental) analysis of the industry shows that the lack of a comprehensive political and regulatory framework still slows down IoT deployment. Interoperability, security, and privacy concerns are additional constraints. Conversely, general economic conditions in most developed and developing economies are favorable to the advancement of IoT technology. Governments are willing to subsidize R&D and have partnered with the private sector to speed up the roll-out process.

IoT Benefits and Growth Opportunities for the Telecom Industry
Key Technology Drivers for Companies

Vincent Sabourin
Jordan Tito Jabo

CRC Press
Taylor & Francis Group
Boca Raton London New York

CRC Press is an imprint of the
Taylor & Francis Group, an **informa** business

First edition published 2023
by CRC Press
6000 Broken Sound Parkway NW, Suite 300, Boca Raton, FL 33487-2742

and by CRC Press
4 Park Square, Milton Park, Abingdon, Oxon, OX14 4RN

CRC Press is an imprint of Taylor & Francis Group, LLC

© 2023 Vincent Sabourin and Jordan Tito Jabo

ISBN: 978-1-032-13314-0 (hbk)
ISBN: 978-1-032-27854-4 (pbk)
ISBN: 978-1-003-29441-2 (ebk)

DOI: 10.1201/9781003294412

Typeset in Times
by SPi Technologies India Pvt Ltd (Straive)

CONTENTS

LIST OF TABLES

LIST OF ABBREVIATIONS

AEP	Application Enablement Platform
API	Application Programming Interface
APL	Application
AVL	Automated Vehicle Location
B2C	Business to Consumer
BaaS	Backend-as-Service
BCE	Bell Canada Enterprises
BM	Business Model
CaaS	Communications as a Service
CAGR	Compound Annual Growth Rate
CEO	Chief Executive Officer
CoAP	Constrained Application Protocol
(CMP)	Connectivity Management Platform
CPU	Central Processing Unit
DM/AEP	Device management/Application Enablement Platform
EIU	The Economist Intelligence Unit
e-SIM	Embedded Subscriber Identification Module
ETSI	The European Telecommunications Standards Institute
EY	Ernest & Young
Gbps	Gigabits per second
GE	General Electric
GPS	Geographical Positioning System
GSM/ CDMA	Global System for Digital Communications/ Code-division Multiple Access
IaaS	Infrastructure-as-Service
IBM	International Business Machine

IDC	International Data Corporation
IdO	Internet des Objets
IEEE	The Institute of Electrical and Electronics Engineers
IERC	International Energy Research Centre
IETF	Internet Engineering Task Force
IoT	Internet of Things
IP	Internet Protocol
IPv6	Internet Protocol Version 6
6LoWPAN	IPv6 Over Low-Power Wireless Personal Area Network
ISA	International Society of Automation
ISO/IEC	International Organization for Standardization/ International Electrotechnical Commission
ITU	International Telecommunication Union
ITU-T	ITU Telecommunication Standardization Sector
LTE	Long-Term Evolution
LTE-M	Long-Term Evolution for Machines
M2M	Machine to Machine
MAC	Medium Access Control
MCU	Microcontrollers
MEMS	Micro-electromechanical systems
MSP	Managed Service Provision
NFC	Near-Field Communication
NWK	Network
O&M	Operations & Maintenance
OTT	Over-the-top
PaaS	Platform-as-Service
PaaS	Platform as service
PESTLE	Political, Economical, Social, Technological, Legal, Environmental
PWC	PricewaterhouseCoopers
QR Code	Quick Response Code
R&D	Research & Development
RFID	Radio-Frequency Identification
SaaS	Software-as-a-Service
SD WAN	Software Defined Wide Area Network
SDO	Standards Development Organizations
US	United States
WEF	World Economic Forum
WSN	Wireless Sensor Networks

Chapter 1

INTRODUCTION AND CHALLENGES FOR THE TELECOM INDUSTRY

1.1 INTRODUCTION

The concept of Internet of Things (IoT) is not very old. It was coined by Kevin Ashton back in 1999 (Ashton, 2009) and featured on Gartner's "hype-cycle for emerging technologies" in 2011 (Fenn and LeHong, 2011). Looking back at history, the concepts of "pervasive computing" and "embedded internet" have been around for some time, and people tend to make analogies between those terms. Even though IoT has not been around for long, the disruptions it has caused to industries are enormous. Industries like health, energy and utilities, retail, transportation, manufacturing, and agriculture have been impacted by the arrival of IoT in a big way. However, this trend does not stop there. Other industries are not immune to the same disruptions IoT has brought about. The Telecom industry has also been hit hard, and impact is visible – positive for those who moved fast to take up opportunities created by IoT and harmful for those who have been slow or lacked means and strategies to follow the trend.

When Gubbi et al. (2013) introduced their article, they mentioned that the next wave in computing would be outside the realm of the traditional desktop. Technological progress has turned ordinary "Things" into intelligent devices. Objects like a watch, thermostat, bulb, meter, camera, and speaker are now more intelligent than ever, thanks to sensors, processors, actuators, and connectivity. The objects otherwise called "Things" have become "Smart" and can interact with people and between themselves, thus generating tons of data, "big data" that are useful to some extent.

This phenomenon is rapidly developing to the extent that some researchers predict that by 2020, connected (smart) objects are estimated at 32 billion worldwide (Adshead, 2014).

DOI: 10.1201/9781003294412-1

The diminishing cost of sensor technology has been a critical factor in expanding Wireless Sensor Networks (WSNs) vital to the development of IoT infrastructure. The diminishing cost of sensor technology has enabled many areas (and industry) such as health and wellness, home and building automation, improved energy efficiency, industrial automation smart metering and smart grid infrastructures, environmental monitoring and forecasting, more flexible RFID infrastructures, asset management and logistics, vehicular automation and intelligent transport, agriculture, smart shopping, (Mainetti et al., 2011) among others, taking advantage to some extent of IoT despite some shortcomings.

Despite the rapid advancement of IoT, security and privacy are excellent sources of concern for IoT development. With billions of connected devices on the network, fear for intruders arises. End users are also unsure how the companies use their data, and laws and regulations are still at their infant stage.

Notwithstanding all these challenges, Telecom has opted or is exploring ways to include IoT in its business models. The spirit of first-mover advantage and the potential of revenue streams from this technology are critical drivers for operators to embrace it.

The Telecom industry has been trying to integrate IoT in its operations to build on the momentum seen in other industries and take advantage of the potential gains it promises; however, many obstacles and constraints are hampering its deployment.

The Telecom industry is infrastructure-intensive and requires enormous investment to re-invent itself and quickly integrate the latest innovations in its strategies. Those innovations concurrently open up business opportunities to other players, including small new, or existing players who eat away on the market share of old players. As digital technology proliferates the telecommunications industry, incumbent Telcos find themselves in the middle of a paradox…. They are, after all, not only providers of their digital products and services but also enablers for other sectors by providing the essential connectivity infrastructure for functioning and growing in the digital economy, which results in a growing demand for broadband access (Meffert and Mohr, 2017).

For example, new players have created over-the-top applications that have replaced some traditional telecom services, gaining some market share at the expense of old players. These players provide services to consumers over the Internet by bypassing traditional distribution channels formerly owned by big telecom companies. Good examples would be Skype, Netflix, YouTube, Xbox 360, and many more. With these innovations, the industry is losing revenues to other players, as has been observed by many scholars.

This book studies telecom companies' business models to catch up on the IoT opportunities. New business models, including IoT, are reviewed for different Canadian telecom companies to highlight their readiness in the market. To better understand the industry vis-à-vis IoT applications, a Political, Economical, Social, Technological, Legal, Environmental (PESTLE) analysis has been carried out in this work. Finally, recommendations have been drawn based on the findings of this book.

1.2 CHALLENGES OF THE INDUSTRY

The primary use of IoT in the Telecom industry has many benefits. IoT can help improve customer experience by tapping into predictive analytics to avoid network outages during peak hours or main events. It can also help monitor and more effectively plan for maintenance to avoid downtimes and loss of revenues. But these are indirect ways telecoms gain from IoT technology. Many companies have IoT projects (products and services in the pipeline) but haven't yet shown their revenue. Many other companies are struggling to integrate IoT into their regular operations. Legacy business models are close to this technological progress and need to be re-opened to include it. They were doing so; a re-design of business models caused a chain reaction on other sub-systems. For example, not many telecom companies have the ready infrastructure to accommodate this new technology. Minimum infrastructure with IoT capabilities has to be laid down. New protocols, platforms, applications, and trained personnel are needed to implement it fully.

1.3 LEVERAGES AND PRESSURE POINTS

The telecommunications industry has gone through difficulties on the one hand, but on the other hand, it has tremendous potential to benefit from IoT development. The amount of data that operators have access to is a treasure trove for the industry. Telcos can predict consumers' behavior and expectations; predictive analytics applied to those data can help avoid network outage; operators can plan and monitor maintenance more effectively and can optimize the bandwidth and coverage according to the patterns and customer behavior; and they can improve customer service with the help of IoT and big data. Apart from this, operators have more opportunities to add services and products to their existing portfolios and create new sources of revenue. Innovation and Research & Development are critical to this kind of move since IoT is relatively new to the industry. However, traditional Telcos have shown to be more rigid and less flexible when integrating this technology. Many people argue that radical innovation is more complex to implement than incremental ones since the former requires time, investments, and changes in the operators' know-how and mindset. Gubbi et al. (2013, p. 1646) define IoT as

a radical evolution of the current Internet into a network of interconnected objects that not only harvests information from the environment (sensing) and interacts with the physical world (actuation/command/control), but also uses existing Internet standards to provide services for information transfer, analytics, applications, and communications.

With IoT, the concept of the Telecom ecosystem has tremendously been altered. The concept has crossed borders to embrace transportation, construction, agriculture, health, insurance, energy, and so many other industries as we have never seen before. Many researchers call it vertical markets, which dynamically change how telecoms create values for their owners.

Collaboration and integration are vital to taking advantage of IoT. However, the Telecom industry has not shown how ready they are to integrate IoT into their daily operations. As a result, shared business models are likely to play a central role in the monetization process of IoT.

Lack of organizational agility is noticed in IoT implementation across the industry, considering how slow it is so far. Moreover, the lack of organizational agility causes a kind of disruptive competition brought upon novel players who affront old industry players.

From a global perspective, Meffert and Mohr (2017) report that Amazon, Apple, Baidu, Google, Microsoft, Samsung, and Tencent, as well as pure tech companies such as Cisco, Huawei, IBM, and ZTE are all growing their presence across the traditional Telecom's value chain with innovative technologies—from network and service through devices and operating systems to applications and media.

Moreover, the same authors say that OTT players offer core Telco services such as voice or messaging, and the media space is becoming their domain. Tech and Internet companies are also increasingly active in growth areas, such as cloud space and services, competing with Telcos for clients and revenues. They are tying customers to their ecosystems while relying on traditional operators, a thing of the past. With carrier-neutral connectivity (e.g., e-SIM), many techs and Internet companies enable seamless changes between operators and eliminate the hassle of changing telecom providers. Hence, digital players are systematically attacking existing Telco profit pools and eating up Telco's revenues and margins. This attack makes differentiation purely on B2C products for traditional Telcos a highly questionable proposition in the future.

In addition to these revenue-eroding trends, regulatory developments—especially in Europe—have dramatically cut down roaming revenues. All told, the opportunities that newcomers, tech, and Internet players are capitalizing on may slow growth for traditional Telcos, costing them upward of $300 billion. Worldwide, the compound annual growth rate (CAGR) for traditional Telcos is estimated at only 0.7% through 2020.

For many Telcos, mainly in developed markets, the outlook is incredibly disappointing with projected negative growth. For example, Telcos in Western Europe and Central and Eastern Europe are facing −1.5 and −1.3% average growth, respectively, over the next four years, while those in North America are expected to barely tread water with growth at only about 0.3% (Meffert and Mohr, 2017).

1.4 OBJECTIVES OF THE BOOK

The objectives of this book are twofold. First, there is a primary objective and then some secondary objectives.

1. Primary objective: The main objective of this book is to carry out a PESTLE analysis of the telecom industry in the era of IoT.
2. Secondary objectives: Secondary objectives are to highlight some of the IoT-based business models in the Telecom industry, assess the impact of IoT on the telecom industry's revenue streams, and identify key IoT technological drivers for the industry.

The following chapters show how these objectives were achieved.

Chapter 2

INTERNET OF THINGS

Perspective and Opportunities for the Telecom Industry

2.1 INTRODUCTION

The literature review chapter intends to shed light on the concepts of Internet of Things (IoT) and the Business Model. Therefore, articles, books, and white papers are reviewed in this chapter to understand the main concepts better. In addition, a synthesis has been done, highlighting the main findings from other authors regarding this topic.

2.2 INTERNET OF THINGS AT A GLANCE

In this section, the concept of IoT is defined, the reasons to embrace IoT are highlighted, and the challenges that come with it are examined.

2.3 THE CONCEPT

The Internet has been around for several decades, and the number of users has not ceased to increase. As a result, many have profited from different Internet applications, products, and uses. The evolution of the use of the Internet is spectacular, and none can deny that it has taken a central role in modern life. More and more aspects of life depend on the Internet nowadays, at least for a significant part, and new uses and applications are being discovered and exploited at high speed. Objects/things that we never thought would be connected to the Internet are now becoming smart and getting connected; the mobility has never been more effortless, the improvement of platforms, speed of bandwidth, and standards for interoperability are easing the development of new Internet applications, leading to new business opportunities we never thought of before. Developments such as cloud computing, analytics, machine learning, big data, and business intelligence are paramount in this regard.

DOI: 10.1201/9781003294412-2

Throughout this evolution of Internet and Internet applications (and, of course of information and communication technologies), the concept of IoT or otherwise called Ubiquitous Internet or Internet of Objects has appeared and shows no sign of slowing down on its implementation and creation of new business opportunities. The International Telecommunication Union (ITU) had predicted this evolution back in 2005 where it said: "We are heading into a new era of ubiquity, where the users" of the Internet are counted in billions and where humans may become the minority as generators and receivers of traffic.

Instead, most traffic flows between devices and all kinds of "things," thereby creating a much broader and more complex "Internet of Things." These "Things" or "objects have specific characteristics that make them useful on the network. Automation seems to be one of the most significant characteristics. For IoT to be helpful, objects must collect data, process them, collaborate with other nodes on the network, and act according to specific protocols.

Businesswise, IoT disrupts some business processes and affects our daily lives, as confirmed by some technology gurus. For example, according to Dell (2017), "IoT is fundamentally changing how we live, how organizations operate, and how the world works." To add on that, Ferber (2013) said: "The IoT, which is often referred to as the internet's next-generation, holds the potential to change our lives with a global system of interconnected computer networks, sensors, actuators, and devices all using the internet protocol." But also, to get to that level, many enablers have to evolve and make the IoT-based expectations happen. In that regard, as put by Westerlund et al. (2014), "IoT represents the future of computing and communication, and the further development of the phenomenon depends on technology innovation in RFID, sensor technologies, smart things/objects, nanotechnology, and miniaturization."

To better understand this concept, we refer to the definitions from various authors.

The ITU has defined IoT as "a global infrastructure for the information society, enabling advanced services by interconnecting (physical and virtual) things based on existing and evolving interoperable information and communication technologies" (Recommendation ITU-T Y.2060).

As to McKinsey's Chui, Löffler, and Roberts (2010) in what's called Internet of Things, sensors and actuators embedded in physical objects—from roadways to pacemakers—are linked through wired and wireless networks, often using the same Internet Protocol (IP) that connects the Internet. These networks churn out huge volumes of data that flow to computers for analysis. When objects can sense the environment and communicate, they become tools for understanding complexity and responding swiftly. Dijkman et al. (2015) say that IoT refers to the interconnection of physical objects by equipping them with sensors, actuators, and a means to connect to the Internet. In its report called Smart China (2009), as put by IBM, every object can be connected in a not distant future. Things can exchange information by themselves, and the number of "things" connected to the Internet is much larger than the number of "people," and humans may become the minority of generators and receivers of traffic. Clearly, the trend shows that human beings are removed from the interaction between machines in the future. Machines are going to talk to machines without people's intervention, which is the concept of IoT. As the ITU Internet Report (2005) points out, a new dimension has been added to the world of information and communication technologies: from any place, connectivity for anyone, we have connectivity for anything.

Defining IoT, Joshi (2016) added that the term is closely identified with RFID as the method of communication, although it also may include other sensor technologies, wireless technologies, or QR codes. IoT is significant because an object that can represent itself digitally becomes something more significant than the object by itself.

Bauer et al. (2014) wrote that IoT refers to the networking of physical objects through embedded sensors, actuators, and other devices that can collect or transmit information about the objects. The data amassed from these devices can then be analyzed to optimize products, services, and operations.

The IERC definition states that IoT is "A dynamic global network infrastructure with self-configuring capabilities based on standard and interoperable communication protocols where physical and virtual" things" have identities, physical attributes, and virtual personalities and use intelligent interfaces, and are seamlessly integrated into the information network."

Gartner defines IoT as the network of physical objects that contain embedded technology to communicate and sense or interact with their internal states or the external environment.

Many authors have suggested different definitions of IoT, but it can generally be defined as a worldwide network of uniquely addressable interconnected objects based on standard communication protocols (Mainetti et al., 2011). All these definitions have some things in common. First, the sensor technology is central to these objects to have a specific value. Smart objects have to have the capabilities to talk to each other without the intervention of a human being through the network.

Since we understand IoT, we can now legitimately ask ourselves how many of those objects are out there in circulation?

From what is known so far, the number of objects/things connected on the Internet is proliferating in the application markets. McKinsey had predicted that by 2020, at least 30 billion objects will be connected as follows:

Nevertheless, another legitimate question would be, what are some examples of vertical markets for IoT?

The most obvious examples of IoT application markets include industrial with factory 4.0, automotive with intelligent parking, homes with intelligent buildings, agricultural with soil analysis, medical with wearable fitness devices, military with threat analysis, environmental with weather prediction, and retail with inventory control. On top of that, there are other markets like energy, education, logistics and transportation, and many more. More detailed IoT application market examples are provided in Appendix 1.

2.4 WHY WOULD ENTERPRISES EMBRACE IoT?

As suggested by Vermesan and Friess (2013), enterprises need to take advantage of three benefits provided by IoT as follows:

- **Increased productivity**—this is at the core of most enterprises and affects the success and profitability of the enterprise.
- **Market differentiation**—in a market saturated with similar products and solutions, it is important to differentiate, and IoT is one of the possible differentiators.
- **Cost efficiency**—reducing the cost of running a business is a "mantra" for most CEOs. Better utilization of resources, better information used in the decision process, or reduced downtime are possible ways to achieve this.

The problem here is how an enterprise can do that without cannibalizing the existing operations. Although obviously, the rationale behind the adoption of IoT differs from enterprise to enterprise, there won't be a universal business model. Every company has its way of creating value using the potential of IoT, mainly because of the diversity of IoT application domains and the different driving forces behind different applications.

2.5 CHALLENGES WITH IoT

IoT still presents many challenges, many of which are barriers to full-scale adoption of this technology. The literature mentions many of them; we can cite those related to security, privacy, and trust. There are others related to interoperability and standardization.

It is expected to see IoT applications in various domains as we showed in the literature, but in the end, those different domains need to collaborate and, in some instances, integrate their applications. But, unfortunately, different administrative and ownership frameworks make users nervous and less confident in exchanging their information across multiple platforms and multiple owners. Therefore, for IoT to succeed, trust has to be built for the users (and all stakeholders) to have that trust and start using IoT services and applications extensively.

There are three broad categories of challenges for IoT. The first category is technical challenges composed of reliability, scaling, and electric power; the second category, policy, comprises cross-border data traffic and legal, regulatory models. Finally, the third category is a mixture of the technical and policy challenges composed of standard & interoperability, privacy & security, and spectrum & bandwidth constraints.

Smooth deployment of IoT and its benefits to Telecom companies depend on how the issues above are resolved across the board. Vermesan and Friess (2013) suggested potential solutions that need to address federation/administrative co-operation as in:

- Heterogeneity and multiplicity of devices and platforms.
- Intuitively usable solutions, seamlessly integrated into the real world.

Talking about the challenges, Brown (2016) added that the privacy issue is also intertwined with legitimate fears about the security vulnerabilities of IoT gear. The best example would be in the home industry. Most commercial home automation systems offer a valuable cloud component for external communications, updates, video storage, voice response, and self-learning analytics. Yet a cloud connection also expands the potential for corporate information harvesting, or even worse, black hats gaining access to the cloud platform to steal personal information or attack systems such as security and heating systems. In response to these vulnerabilities, many open source automation projects promote a localized approach where you control your cloud, even if it's at the expense of extended functionality.

Chapter 3

INTERNET OF THINGS IN THE TELECOM INDUSTRY
A Survey of Transformation Trends

One of the objectives of this book was to conduct a PESTLE analysis of the Telecom industry about Internet of Things (IoT) to understand better the current environment in which IoT is being rolled out. This chapter aims to highlight IoT-based business models in the Telecom industry, assess the impact of IoT on the telecom industry's revenue streams, carry out a PESTLE analysis of the industry about IoT, and identify its critical technological drivers.

The goal of this analysis is twofold. First, to identify the environment in which a company operates; second, to collect data and valuable information which may help a company to predict future situations, problems, and opportunities (Yüksel, 2012).

Our analysis of the disruptive innovation related to the telecom sector touches on the factors that lead to a redefinition of the competitive landscape and phenomena of disintermediation for communication utilities. These factors are opening strategic windows for introducing new business models enabled by IoT. This research employs PESTLE analysis to extensively assess the macro-environment position of IoT in the Telecom sector.

3.1 CONTEXT

The concept of IoT is not very old. It was coined by Kevin Ashton back in 1999 (Ashton, 2009) and featured on Gartner's "hype-cycle for emerging technologies" in 2011 (Fenn and LeHong, 2011). This phenomenon is rapidly developing to the extent that some researchers predict that by 2020, connected (smart) objects are estimated at 32 billion worldwide (Adshead, 2014).

DOI: 10.1201/9781003294412-3

The diminishing cost of sensor technology has been a critical factor in expanding Wireless Sensor Networks (WSNs) vital to the development of IoT infrastructure. These diminishing costs have enabled many areas (and industry) such as health and wellness, home and building automation, improved energy efficiency, industrial automation smart metering and smart grid infrastructures, environmental monitoring and forecasting, more flexible RFID infrastructures, asset management and logistics, vehicular automation and intelligent transport, agriculture, smart shopping (Mainetti et al., 2011), among others, taking advantage at some extent of IoT despite some shortcomings.

Despite the rapid advancement of IoT, security and privacy are excellent sources of concern for IoT development. With billions of connected devices on the network, fear for intruders arises. End users are also unsure how the companies use their data, and laws and regulations are still at their infant stage.

Notwithstanding all these challenges, many industries, including Telecom, have opted or are exploring ways to include IoT in their business models. The spirit of first-mover advantage and the potential of revenue streams from this technology are critical drivers for operators to embrace it.

The Telecom industry has been trying to integrate IoT in its operations to build on the momentum seen in other industries and take advantage of the potential gains it promises; however, many obstacles and constraints are hampering this effort.

The Telecom industry is infrastructure-intensive and requires enormous investment to reinvent itself and quickly integrate the latest innovations in its strategies. Those innovations concurrently open up business opportunities to other players, including small new or existing players who eat away on the market share of old players. As digital transformation proliferates the telecommunications industry, incumbent Telcos find themselves in the middle of a paradox. They are, after all, not only providers of their digital products and services but also enablers for other sectors, providing the essential connectivity infrastructure for functioning and growing in the digital economy, which results in a growing demand for broadband access (Meffert and Mohr, 2017).

For example, new players have created over-the-top applications that have replaced some traditional telecom services, gaining some market share at the expense of old players. These players provide services to consumers over the Internet by bypassing traditional distribution channels formerly owned by big telecom companies. Good examples would be Skype, Netflix, YouTube, Xbox 360, and many more.

In the Internet of Things Business Index 2017 published by The Economist Intelligence Unit (EIU) in 2017, most executives surveyed believe that following an IoT technology path is crucial to their long-term success (The Economist Intelligence Unit, 2018). This shared understanding about the future digital products and services among executives results from the growing trend for many businesses adopting IoT to make their operations more effective and efficient and diversify their revenue streams (Markets and Markets, 2017). In the Telecom industry, with globally declining margins coupled with competition from non-traditional Telecom operators like OTTs, it is imperative to consider other opportunities to remain competitive and profitable (Andersson and Mattsson, 2015). IoT is a crucial driver of the digital transformation that enables businesses to reinvent products, services, internal operations, and business models, as argued by the Economist Intelligence Unit (2017). The ever-wider availability of technologies such as mobile, artificial intelligence, cloud, analytics, and platforms is dramatically altering the way we live, work, and interact—in what has been termed the Fourth Industrial Revolution (Dong-Hee and Yong, 2017).

The findings of this chapter are discussed under 28 observations which are summarized in Table 3.1—Summary at the end of this chapter: 28 Trends-based PESTLE Analysis for IoT in the Telecom Industry. The factors have been highlighted under each of the factors under research.

3.2 POLITICAL FACTORS

The political environment plays a crucial role in shaping the strategic context of IoT for the telecom industry. We have observed five trends for this environment: promotion and education, political stability, political risks and regulations, and trade barriers.

Governments worldwide are keen on promoting IoT use and committed subsidies to IoT-related R&D and the implementation of IoT solutions. Our research has established that governments around the globe have a great interest in creating environments that can foster the growth of IoT. Some of the governments are heavily promoting the use of IoT and are committed to setting aside subsidies to enable IoT related R&D to thrive (Weber, 2013). Implementation of IoT is no

TABLE 3.1

Trends-Based PESTLE Analysis for IoT in the Telecom Industry

Political	1.	Governments around the world are keen on promoting the use of IoT and committed subsidies to IoT-related R&D and the implementation of IoT solutions.
	2.	Politically stable environment in developed countries as well as some developing countries will be key in IoT adoption worldwide.
	3.	Traditional political risks for Telecom related to regulations, network licensing, national radio spectrums and in case of certain nations trade barriers will affect IoT deployment.
	4.	Political risks rooted in national security and human rights issues will prevail in the IoT era.
	5.	Trade barriers resulting from some protectionist policies in some countries will hinder IoT business.
Economic	6.	Good economic health in the largest world economies such as the USA and China.
	7.	Although Telecom's revenues have recently stagnated or even declined in some parts of the world, Telecoms can still leverage their existing infrastructure for IoT implementation.
Social	8.	Some individuals are still reluctant to embrace IoT products and services because of fear of privacy violation and data security.
	9.	Millennials are likely to quickly understand the IoT concept and embrace it more easily.
	10.	Consumer buying patterns in the developed world demonstrate that technology-based products and services are gaining momentum.
	11.	Media have tremendously covered the IoT phenomenon helping for the social awareness about it.
	12.	The use of smartphones has grown worldwide, making it easier to deploy smart applications and allow owners to use IoT solutions wherever they are.
	13.	A larger number of people around the world are growing health conscious and are using some IoT solutions like smartwatches and wrist bands to track their physical activity contributing to IoT awareness and acceptance among consumers.

(Continued)

TABLE 3.1 *(Continued)*

Technological	14. Telecoms have the technological know-how that they can build on to deploy IoT solutions.
	15. IoT phenomenon is still at infant phase, more R&D and promotion efforts still needed for large-scale acceptance and adoption.
	16. Competing technologies to traditional Telecom such as OTTs affect the ways of creating and capturing value for Telecoms.
	17. IPv6, 5G networks, cloud computing, and mobile computing are enablers of IoT and are for the part being used around the world.
	18. Needs for autonomous driving, smart cities, wearables, smart health, smart transportation…make IoT technology spread in all people's walks of life.
	19. Massive deployment of sensors, analytics, and machine-learning as an opportunity for Telecoms to seize.
	20. Network quality remains a key point of differentiation.
Legal	21. In-market consolidation (M&A) is the leading driver for the industry.
	22. Uniform standards across the world are still an issue despite efforts to develop and uniformalize them.
	23. Many countries haven't yet put in place regulations that will guide the industry. Sporadic laws and rules are still a fragment of what is needed to regulate this new area.
	24. Laws regarding privacy, security, etc. will impact the IoT roll out.
Environmental	25. E-waste issue is still an issue for the industry. Waste management, device recycling and minimization of environment footprint will have to be considered.
	26. Possible environmental activists' pressure on the industry may affect the overall cost of the products/services.
	27. Products using green energy (Ex. solar energy) and/or low power consumption will reduce the environmental impact of IoT.
	28. The need to reduce energy consumption and toxic emission will continue to drive IoT in the smart cities, smart building, smart transportation, etc.

longer a concern of the private sector but a country investment agenda across many economies (Buttarelli, 2010).

A politically stable environment in developed countries and some developing countries is critical in IoT adoption worldwide. Political stability is an excellent element that ensures the growth of any industry and innovation. With this factor, Vermesan et al. (2011) argue that emerging economies have embraced a spirit of creating stability within their economies to attract investment and goodwill from investors. A politically stable environment in developed countries and some developing countries are thus the keys in IoT adoption globally (Dutton, 2014).

In the last decade, some economies have had rough times, which have resulted from political risk. Such risks have emerged from internal regulations and industrial interest in creating open networks that thrive interoperability. According to Mani and Chouk (2017), traditional political risks for Telecom related to regulations, network licensing, national radio spectrums, and certain nations' trade barriers significantly affect IoT deployment.

With the growth of IoT, countries are also keen to bolster their internal security systems. According to Haghi et al. (2017), this is due to fear of cyber-related crimes in which hackers are likely to launch against the security systems. Thus, as Dutton (2014) argues, political risks rooted in national security and human rights issues prevail in IoT era if relevant stakeholders take great care.

Kim et al. (2012) assert that countries also take precautions to protect their industries against external entry. According to Vermesan and Friess (2014), this is especially important as it concerns infant companies in the telecom sector, where extensive and well-developed players may hinder their growth and take-off. Therefore, it is essential to note that trade barriers resulting from some protectionist policies in some countries hinder IoT business, as Direction (2015) argued.

3.3 ECONOMIC ENVIRONMENT

For any innovation to grow and achieve its full exploitation in the market, it must operate in a stable economic environment. According to Mani and Chouk (2017), excellent and sound economic policies can attract investors, thus encouraging investment. As argued by European Commission (2013), essential to note, there is good economic health in the most significant world economies such as China and the USA.

Kingsley et al. (2012) also note that companies operating in volatile and economically challenged spaces must create robust business development plans and strategies to generate incremental revenues. Being innovative and highly dynamic in the market could also help telecoms to maintain their profitability in the long run. However, Although Telecom's revenues have recently stagnated or even declined in some parts of the world, Telecoms can still leverage their existing infrastructure for IoT implementation.

3.4 SOCIAL FACTORS

Some of the leading Internet-enabled tech companies, such as Facebook, have been accused and penalized for violating the privacy of their clients (Arthur, 2018). The fear of personal data breach and violation of customer privacy places IoT adoption in the telecom sector precarious. According to Bork and Sidak, some consumers are still reluctant to embrace IoT products and services because of fear of privacy violation and data security.

As complemented by existing research, Markets and Markets (2017) has indicated that millennials and the emerging generation are likely to embrace IoT as a new technology due to their technological experimentation appetite. Moreover, since most of the global population is composed of young consumers who are technologically empowered, there is an opportunity to drive consumer awareness related to IoT in the telecom sector. According to Bharati, Zhang, and Chaudhury, this is due to millennials understanding IoT concept fast and embracing it more easily.

Researchers continue to excite the market by reporting that consumer buying behaviors drive the growth of technology shortly (Claudy et al., 2015). According to Mani and Chouk (2017), developed economies have been described as having consumers with a readiness mindset to embrace new technology. Oh and Teo (2010) claim that consumer buying patterns in the developed world show that technology-based products and services are gaining momentum. This momentum is being fuelled by buyers being ready to adopt these technologies despite the challenges that come with them (Dutton, 2014).

Social media platforms are the levers emerging companies can use to create more trials for their products in the market. For instance, Facebook runs on an Internet-enabled platform that telecom companies provide (Market and Markets, 2017). Therefore, these media platforms, such as Facebook, become a significant market where players can partner to create synergy and achieve faster market routes with solid consumer solutions. Furthermore, Raffaele et al. assert that media houses have tremendously covered IoT phenomenon by creating sustainable social awareness about it.

It is not always easy to achieve technological success without the correct drivers. In that regard, smartphones have grown worldwide to become a significant technology enabler (Porter, 2014). The key to note in this concept is that smartphones have made it easier to deploy intelligent applications and enable phone owners to use IoT applications anywhere anytime (Dong-Hee and Yong Jin, 2017).

There is a growing concern among global consumers regarding the consumption of health-conscious products (Kang et al., 2015). A more significant part of the global population has now embraced IoT solutions and innovations such as smartwatches and wrist bands to monitor their physical activities. Being health conscious quickly contributes to IoT awareness and faster acceptance by consumers.

3.5 TECHNOLOGICAL SECTOR

One of the unique value propositions that telecom companies have is their technical capability. Many of these companies have years of experience in the industry and have solved multifaceted and highly dynamic challenges, making them quite versatile to modern challenges (Dong-Hee and Yong Jin, 2017). According to Raffaele et al., telecoms have the technological know-how that they can thus build on to deploy IoT solutions.

IoT as an innovation though quite promising, must be carefully evaluated in cost–benefit analysis. This cost–benefit analysis helps establish its actual viability state and level of attractiveness, which may help investors to plan for considerable investment into the industry. According to Markets and Markets (2017), the IoT phenomenon is still at the infant phase; more R&D and promotion efforts are still needed for large-scale acceptance and adoption.

Any industry player must continually create and capture value from the investors' resources (Gubbi et al., 2013). This value creation implies that emerging technologies must create a new blend into the industry and should not come in as competitors. According to Dong-Hee and Yong Jin (2017), competing technologies to traditional Telecom such as OTTs create and capture value for telecoms.

This research has also established that for telecom sectors to thrive, they must consistently impact their consumers (Oh and Teo, 2010).

The level of consistency should focus on the levels of innovation, levels of continuous improvements in their infrastructure based on the emerging demand and consumer base (Claudy et al., 2015). Mani and Chouk (2017) report that IPv6, 5G networks, cloud computing, and mobile computing are enablers of IoT and are used worldwide. With technological advancement and innovation, consumers beg to form a mindset that engenders modernity and technological complexities (Claudy et al., 2015). For instance, companies have developed self-customized gadgets such as autonomous cars and intelligent buildings through co-piloting. According to Haghi et al. (2017), the current consumer needs for autonomous driving, smart cities, wearables, innovative health, and intelligent transportation would spread IoT technology in all people's walks of life.

3.6 LEGAL ENVIRONMENT

In the telecommunication sector, companies have become more strategic in their operations. Instances of in-market consolidation (M&A) are the leading drivers for the industry. Emerging companies are fast merging with the incumbent to gain faster entry into the industry and at the same time benefit from critical resources such as technology, innovation, and talent (Markets and Markets, 2017).

Industry standardization in any economy drives the stability of the whole industry in the economy. Ensuring uniformity in the industry also ensures that players can only operate within set regulatory standards. However, a key challenge is that uniform standard worldwide is still an issue despite efforts to develop and formalize them (Kingsley et al., 2012).

Having an innovation merge with existing technology, IoT, and the telecom sector is a new challenge to many countries (European Commission, 2013). Some economies are trying to put structures and policies to ensure that innovations and technologies are carried out competently. However, many countries haven't yet put regulations that guide the industry. As a result, sporadic laws and rules are still a fragment of what is needed to regulate this new area.

As the industry of telecom sector continues to grow, challenges of sustainable laws and regulations are fast emerging. The embracement of IoT likely affects how companies collect and use personal information and how such information is protected against any misuse. Hence, according to Andersson and Mattsson (2015), laws regarding privacy and security, impact how IoT is rolled out within the telecom sector.

3.7 ENVIRONMENTAL FACTORS

Waste management is an issue that is negatively impacting the telecom sector. With the drive to move to a digital footprint, the telecom sector faces the challenge of identifying, sorting, and managing persistent waste disposal in the industry (Coetzee and Eksteen, 2011). There is high pressure from industry activists directed at technology players to ensure that these technologies are safe and environmentally friendly. Such pressure becomes a cost, which should be provided for in the company financial statements. Singh (2010) offers to explains this concept by reporting that any possible environmental activists' pressure on the telecom industry may affect the overall cost of the products/services.

Driving down the impact of technology on the environment can only become possible if players adopt a clean energy policy. Most industry players are fast developing alternative sources of energy that have less or no impact on the environment. Hence, according to Bonardi and van den Bergh (2015), products using green energy, such as solar energy and those with low power consumption, help reduce the impact of IoT on the environment.

According to industry practitioners, there is a greater need to fully commission green energy that can be harnessed by IoT intelligent applications to help create a unique balance of maintaining a clean, habitable environment. In addition, industry activists and consumer groups have exerted pressure pushing telecom companies to adopt intelligent applications in their operations. The need to reduce energy consumption and toxic emission thus continues to drive IoT applications in smart cities, intelligent buildings, and intelligent transportation.

3.8 CHANGE DRIVERS AND THE IMPACT ON THE TELECOM INDUSTRY

The growing market of IoT represents a business opportunity for stakeholders. IoT provides myriad new services and business opportunities and helps companies create new value (Hui, 2014). Companies need to strategically rethink their current business model to dominate the emerging IoT market. However, many companies have difficulty developing IoT business models because IoT-driven market dynamics are not explicit in the model (Turber and Smiela, 2014).

Yet, successful IoT implementations are not just the result of technology innovation but involve the intelligently coordinated innovation of products, services, and business models (Berthelsen, 2015). The entire IoT domain is demanding new service concepts and business models, as companies need to "fundamentally rethink their orthodoxies about value creation and value capture" (Hui, 2014). This kind of transformation requires converting from a product to a service mindset (Hui, 2014; Dahlberg et al., 2015). A significant challenge for IoT-related projects in realizing the business potential is the integration of multiple businesses operating in collaborative environments (Glova et al., 2014).

For Telecoms to create and capture the value of IoT, they need to overhaul their legacy business models. Several key technology factors impact their product scope, market scope, geographical scope, and scope of competence.

IoT is a thing now. Nevertheless, several issues still have to be addressed from a technical to regulatory standpoint. In this article, we discuss the external macro environment of the Telecom sector regarding IoT technology with the help of PESTLE analysis.

We show that the telecom sector is progressively transformed by new technologies, including IoT. As a result, several IoT-enabled products and services are being marketed, and estimates of its potential market are enticing.

Like any other new technology, the general public acceptance of IoT depends on how secure the end user feels about it and how policymakers and businesses partner effectively to enact, promote, and enforce good policies, regulations, and security. Tremendous progress has been made, but the technology is still fragmented, with companies and countries developing their standards. Global collaboration ensures harmonized and standardized development, which is key to interoperability across industries. Without interoperability, it is hard and even impossible to unleash the full potential of IoT for the telecom sector.

Part of the Telecom infrastructure is outdated and needs an upgrade to sustain the new technologies, but still, it offers great hope to companies to take up opportunities as first movers and build upon them. The upgrade of the infrastructure or even the construction of a new one compatible with the 5G protocol is paramount for the operators to accept many IoT devices on their respective networks and benefit from it. The IPv6 came at the right time and enabled an "unlimited" number of devices that are key to IoT development.

As discussed here above, declining margins for Telecoms needed to be refueled. IoT is to the telecom companies what energy is to the car to continue running and achieve their target bottom line. However, no one can do it all. Telecoms need partnerships with other players to quickly integrate IoT technology into their business models. For example, Telecoms do not manufacture IoT-enabled devices, sensors, and actuators and need to work closely with reliable manufacturers to deliver those devices to end users quickly and cost-effectively. As usual, part of the job continues to be outsourced to minimize cost while speeding up delivery. In the IoT era, Telecoms need to strategically rethink their value proposition and ensure IoT adds to their revenue streams by reimagining how human beings communicate among themselves, how they interact with things, and how things communicate among themselves. Today, there are so many substitutes on the market for some or even most products and services that once were the monopoly of traditional sector players. New players like the over-the-top media service providers have entered the market and are eating away at the market share of old players by taking advantage of the digital transformation of the telecom operations. The icing on the cake changes in the customer relationship that needs to be implemented. Educating traditional customers on the benefits of IoT-enabled products/services has to be on the top of the players' agenda. Even though millennials and Gen Y are tech-savvy and are among early adopters of this technology, members of Gen X are still the driving force of the market as they occupy strategic positions in many companies that generally are consumers of technologies.

As discussed in the PESTLE analysis of this article, governments have a huge role to play in collaboration with the private sector at this stage of development. Many researchers have highlighted examples of governments' investments in R&D, but they need to go beyond that to ensure the general public benefit from this technology in different ways without fear of security threats and privacy intrusions. The fact that technology-based products and services have gained momentum on the market should not make Telecoms and policymakers forget that mass adoption of IoT-enabled products and services depends upon the general population's acceptance after all fears and cost-related issues have been cleared. Health-conscious customers who adopt IoT-enabled products like smartwatches and wrist bands play an important role in raising awareness among the general public but should not blindfold players and forget to deal with customers' concerns and promote this technology at a larger scale.

3.9 CONCLUDING REMARKS

This chapter has established that IoT in the telecom sector is a very dynamic and vibrant business sector that holds the potential for colossal market growth. The expected compound annual growth rate for IoT adoption in Telecom over the coming years is 15.1 %, clearly demonstrating the rapid growth of this crucial technology sector (Markets and Markets, 2017). Furthermore, significant growth is expected in intelligent energy management, intelligent communication technologies, IoT-based optical communications based on real time (Ritola et al., 2015). These innovations are primarily driven by opening space for the political environment, economic opportunities and investment, social factors, technological growth, legal environment, and environmental consciousness with stricter preferences for greener and cheaper technology solutions. Therefore, IoT in the telecom sector provides competitive advantages to vital telecommunication industries in Canada and the rest of the world economies (Ritola et al., 2015).

The above-stated facts inexorably affect Telecoms' business models scrambling to take up the opportunities brought about by IoT. Classic Telecom business models are not able to seize these opportunities. Yet again, these devices (sensors and actuators) and the new types of digital businesses are using Telecom's networks. For example, PWC (2015) estimated that OTT TV is the digital turning point for the TV industry. It affects business models and success factors along with all the steps of the value chain of the TV industry, from content creation to distribution. Therefore, all the players in the TV industry need to determine their strategy to deal with this transformation. Speed and agility in reshaping the strategy are critical success factors because the pace of the transformation is picking up, and many players are taking new positions.

While OTT media distribution practice is widespread among young consumers and looks attractive to Telecom operators, considering the growing revenue streams, it is crucial to avoid cannibalizing existing services. Products and services must not exclude one another. Therefore, interoperability within the widening product scope for telecoms is paramount. In their mapping of the IoT value, McKinsey Global Institute (2015) found that interoperability between IoT systems is critically important to capturing maximum value; on average, interoperability is required for 40% of potential value across IoT applications and by nearly 60% in some settings.

The report further states that interoperability is required to unlock more than $4 trillion per year in potential economic impact from IoT use in 2025, out of a total potential impact of $11.1 trillion across the nine settings analyzed. There are several ways Telecoms can achieve this, including adopting open standards or implementing platforms/ solutions that allow different IoT systems to communicate with one another. Furthermore, with consumers becoming more and more educated about technologies, they doubtlessly consider this while selecting solutions available on the market. Therefore, solution providers must not overwhelm the consumer with too many IoT devices and systems that cannot be synched and generate a large volume of data impossible to manage for an average consumer who needs more accessible solutions to deploy.

Chapter 4

IoT NEW BUSINESS MODELS AND THE DIGITAL TRANSFORMATION OF THE TELECOM INDUSTRY

4.1 DEFINITION

> *A product is the center of a business model, but it is not a business in and of itself–it can't succeed without a great business model.*
>
> *(The Dragon's Den Guide to Real-World Business Models)*

From the quote above, it is clear that designing a good business model (BM) is essential to its strategy. Companies rely on their BMs to deliver and achieve their bottom line. Today, the business world is highly driven by the development and high utilization of information and communication technologies that make them do business or make decisions in real time. These technologies significantly influence how products are designed, how services are delivered, and how BMs are designed. Moreover, these technologies open up new opportunities for innovative products, services, and BMs for those keen on integrating them or taking advantage of their offer.

Timmers (1998) defined a BM as "an architecture of products, services, and information flow...". Negelmann (2001) added that

> a business model defines and structures the fundamental way and form of the aspired added value of a firm. In addition, it contains the description of the exchange processes, the roles of the participants, the profits for business partners as well as the revenue sources to be realized.

DOI: 10.1201/9781003294412-4

Examining the above definitions, Glova et al. (2014) argue that a BM is an abstraction of the complexity of a company by reducing it to its core elements and their interrelations, which facilitates the analysis and the description of business activities. On the other hand, de Man (2012) said a BM describes the rationale of creating value or, as a part of it, making money. But this description usually does not take the form of a structure model.

Many definitions have been given to the concept of BM, but the complete definition would be the one given by Osterwalder and Pigneur (2010), who suggested: "A business model describes the rationale of how an organization creates, delivers, and captures value." According to the authors, a good BM has got nine building blocks.

As the authors point out, a total of nine building blocks should be seen in a good BM. Partner networks, key activities, offers, customer relationships, customer segments, essential resources, distribution channels, cost structure, and revenue streams. These elements look like a general idea about the BM at the surface, but it has much to tell about what BM Telecoms should build to gain from IoT. Any IoT product/service can be evaluated using this model. If we take an example of a company that has an IoT product for smart homes, they should be able to define who is their partner, what is their offer to the customer, what is the relationship with customers, who is the target customer, what are their distribution channels, what are their costs and revenue streams.

To further describe a BM, many authors have introduced the concept of the BM framework (Osterwalder and Pigneur (2010), Johnson et al. (2008), Gordijn (2002)) which is a mental model for thinking about BMs.

4.2 ROLE OF A BUSINESS MODEL IN BUSINESS

A BM comes before a business plan. A BM is the best tool that tells the strengths and the weaknesses of a business idea, essential to decide whether to take a step further and invest more time and capital in the business idea at hand. A good BM can be considered a tool to assess the business concept in the entrepreneur's mind. Usually, a BM needs to pass two basic tests: the narrative and the numbers tests. The first tells whom the business works for, the potential customers, and the estimated value. The second test ensures that the idea generates a profit, not a loss, by comparing the cost and benefit assumptions. It is rare for the business idea to succeed if it did not pass both tests initially.

In the era of information technology, firms keep imagining new ways of doing things and creating value for the owners. Technology has been an accelerator toward that approach. This approach often engenders promising innovations that give great products/services to be commercialized or add value to the existing products/services. Firms innovate in the fields of their existing businesses. However, some other firms proceed to acquisitions on just innovative products/ services that fall outside of their fields of experience, with the idea of diversification or horizontal integration. Interestingly, Chesbrough and Rosenbloom (2002) point out that "the technological management literature shows that firms have great difficulty managing innovations that fall outside of their previous experience, where their earlier beliefs and practices do not apply." Finally, there comes the role of the BM.

In this regard, a good BM is needed to shed light on the new business idea or innovation areas for the managers to implement it effectively and efficiently. For example, managers need to know that "the business model provides a coherent framework. These business models take technological characteristics and potentials as inputs, and converts them through customers and markets into economic outputs" and

> firms need to understand the cognitive role of the business model, to commercialize the technology in a way that allows firms to capture value from their technology investments when opportunities presented by its technologies do not fit well with the firm's current business model.
>
> (Chesbrough and Rosenbloom, 2002)

Spencer and Ayoub (2014) added that "Since the business model drives individuals' working relationships, accountability and goals, it thereby defines roles, expectations and organizational identities."

4.3 IoT-SPECIFIC BUSINESS MODELS FOR TELECOM INDUSTRY

General BMs exist that combine the nine blocks as explained in Section 4.1. In this section, we look at IoT-specific ones for the Telecom industry. As suggested by Qingjun at Huawei (2018), Table 4.1 presents the IoT BM for telecom industry and the six BMs.

There exist six possible IoT BMs for telecom operators. Most models rely on the existing infrastructure. However, some aspects of

TABLE 4.1
IoT Business Model for Telecom Industry and the Six Business Models

Business Model	Name of BM	Description
Business Model 1	IaaS	This model is the traditional M2M market. Operators sell SIM cards, but don't know where or in what scenarios they're used, and provide only general network guarantees and billing functionality. This very simple approach uses a data package sales model.
Business Model 2	PaaS	The operator constructs a Connectivity Management Platform (CMP) for the IoT market, providing SIM card management services and offering customer-facing services like self-service allowance queries and top-ups, and volume activation/shutdown. At this stage, the operator can also adopt a message-based billing method as well as the traditional one based on data usage. Because CMP provides a link to industry customers, operators can package cloud services on top of connectivity services and also move into the module market.
Business Model 3	PaaS+	This typical platform model includes building an AEP that lets operators integrate Communications as a Service (CaaS) capabilities, like voice, SMS, video calls, and data storage, with third-party capabilities, such as voice semantic identification/control, image recognition, and maps. The operator can open these capabilities to developers and industry customers through cloud APIs. In addition to a billing model based on data usage or messages, customers can be billed according to API invocations or functions packages.
Business Model 4	SaaS	The operator builds general-purpose industry suites by refining solutions for common industry requirements. Customers just need to do a small amount of development and customization to meet specific needs for different scenarios like smart homes, smart metering, or warehouse management. The billing model can be based on either the number of connected devices or the industry suite.

(Continued)

TABLE 4.1 *(Continued)*

Business Model	Name of BM	Description
Business Model 5	SaaS+	Similar to Model 4, but with an extra layer. The carrier provides connectivity as well as device and upper-layer application platforms, realizing the E2E integration of upstream and downstream ends of the chain. It participates in industry back-end O&M through service provision. By generating value for industry customers, the operator can acquire even higher returns and participate in value distribution through revenue sharing. This model suits new application scenarios in small-scale industries that are easier to enter but offer high value.
Business Model 6	BaaS	Backend-as-service: This is the most advanced form of industry application. The operator obtains a business license and operates in a cross-sector manner.

Source: Adapted from Qingjun (2018).

these models have been in place for quite some time by IoT rollout. For example, cloud computing services typically fall into three groups: Software-as-a-Service (SaaS) providing applications via the Internet (e.g., www.salesforce.com), Platform-as-a-Service (PaaS) supporting software developers through the whole software life-cycle (development, test, and deployment) (e.g., www.windowsazure. com), and Infrastructure-as-a-Service providing necessary infrastructure by which organizations would not need to purchase servers, datasets and network resources (e.g., www.gogrid.com) (Jadeja and Modi, 2012).

The quick adoption of cloud computing has been behind the birth of the software-as-a-service (SaaS) concept. Automatic management of clouds for hosting and delivering IoT services as SaaS (Software-as-a-Service) applications will be the integrating platform of the Future Internet (Gubbi et al., 2013). In the IoT and cloud computing era, it does not surprise many to see the SaaS become part of many operators' BMs. Intelligent applications for bright things started to count as another product fueling the change of Telecoms' BMs to create and capture the value of IoT.

Qingjun (2018) recommends the following three BMs: Model 2 (connection specialist), Model 3 (platform provider), and Model 5 (solutions provider) for Telecom operators. This section highlights different BMs that telecom operators can choose from to implement IoT-oriented solutions, most of which leverage the existing capabilities with the Telecom companies. Integrating IoT in operations would be made feasible by the expertise, means, and infrastructure companies that have been building for years. Therefore, the remaining question would be, is it necessary for Telecoms to integrate IoT in their operations? The following section addresses this fundamental question.

4.4 THE COMPELLING NEED TO INTEGRATE IoT IN THE TELECOM BUSINESS MODELS

Section 4.3 presented different BM for telecom operators. A good question raised is whether companies need to integrate IoT in their operation. This section answers that question and explains why IoT should be a centerpiece of Telecoms' BMs.

In the Internet of Things Business Index 2017 published by The Economist Intelligence Unit (EIU) in 2017, most executives surveyed believe that following an IoT technology path is crucial to their long-term success. This shared understanding about the future digital products and services among executives results from the growing trend for many businesses adopting IoT to make their operations more effective and efficient and diversify their revenue streams.

In the Telecom industry, with globally declining margins coupled with competition from non-traditional Telecom operators like OTTs, it is imperative to consider other opportunities to remain competitive and profitable. Internet of Things (IoT) is a crucial driver of the digital transformation that enables businesses to reinvent products, services, internal operations, and BMs, says The Economist Intelligence Unit (2017). The ever-wider availability of mobile, artificial intelligence, cloud, analytics, and platforms are dramatically altering the way we live, work, and interact—in what has been termed the Fourth Industrial Revolution.

The telecommunications (Telecom) industry is playing a critical role in enabling this digital revolution to unfold around us (World Economic Forum (WEF), 2017). The WEF report (2017) further adds that the industry faces a rapidly changing economic and competitive landscape driven by internal and external digital disruptions. So far, telecom operators' role in accelerating digital business and service models has not translated into new value for the operators themselves. Operators' share of the industry profit pool has declined from 58% in 2010 to 47% in 2015. This estimate is forecast to drop to 45% in 2018. Pressure on traditional revenues means that it is increasingly important for operators to look at new digital BMs to share digital transformation value.

Nevertheless, the future looks promising for those who see and seize an opportunity in digital transformation. The report (WEF, 2017) also mentions that the digital transformation of telecommunications represents a $2 trillion opportunity for industry and society. As not-so-common competitors like OTTs service providers enter the market and eat away at the industry's revenues and profitability, incumbent operators need to build networks for the future and look beyond the pipe. IoT is being said to be the catalyst of the fourth industrial revolution.

Unfortunately, the current state of affairs is not sustainable for the Telecom industry and needs to be revisited. McKinsey Global Institute (2015) argues that:

> Today's cellular phone networks are not well equipped to handle the demands of the Internet of Things. IoT applications require a great deal of data capacity and are less expensive than current mobile voice or data services. Moreover, IoT devices need to work on low power. Telecom service providers that can deliver lower-cost and lower-energy communication services have a distinct advantage in serving the growing IoT market. However, simply providing communications services is likely to become a commodity business. So, to capture a disproportionate share of IoT value, telecom providers likely have to go beyond their horizontal platform roots by investing in other levels of technology and developing vertical knowledge to create solutions.

Objects around us are getting smarter thanks to sensors, actuators, and intelligent applications. These objects are being connected to the network for communication purposes, but, at the same time, they generate tons of data—big data—that are worth billions of dollars. However, new skill sets like data analytics are crucial to monetizing these IoT data swamps. This new skill set brings us to explore the key drivers and their impact on Telecom's BMs in terms of product scope, market scope, geographical scope as well as the competence scope.

4.5 KEY TECHNOLOGICAL DRIVERS OF IoT AND THEIR IMPACT ON THE TELECOM BUSINESS MODELS

This section explores the vital technological drivers of IoT and their potential to transform the way. As a result, telecom companies conduct their business by rethinking, creating, and capturing value.

IoT is proliferating, expanding into different industries from manufacturing to health, transport, and building to wearables. As a result, an excellent financial incentive is critical for businesses to adopt this technology and transform themselves accordingly. The Economist Intelligent Unit (2013) argues that the most significant incentive for businesses to move ahead with IoT is arguably the potential financial returns from its "productization."

4.5.1 Widespread Wireless Connectivity

The first identified driver is widespread wireless connectivity. This widespread wireless connectivity significantly impacts the telecoms' BMs in a way or another. As put by Kortuem et al. (2010), the Future Internet aims to integrate heterogeneous communication technologies, both wired and wireless, to contribute substantially to assert the concept of IoT. The low cost of sensor technology has eased the proliferation of Wireless Sensor Networks (WSNs) in many applicative scenarios such as environmental monitoring, agriculture, healthcare, and intelligent buildings (Mainetti et al., 2011). Even though the amount of data transferred from/to a single sensor or actuator is minimal, the overall amount of data could be huge due to many objects and their frequent interaction (Lee and Crespi, 2011).

Nodes on the WSNs are intelligent objects. These objects are battery-operated, which causes another critical aspect of power consumption. Different solutions for effective communication of the smart objects are being developed; some of them are presented in Section 4.5.2. According to Vineela and Mezeer (2015), the application requirements for low cost, a high number of sensors, fast deployment, long lifetime, low maintenance, and high quality of service are considered in the specification and design of the platform and all its components. That way, the end users can create applications mixing real-world devices such as home appliances with virtual services on the Web. This type of application is often referred to as physical mashups (Kovatsch et al., 2010). Some technologies and standards developed to facilitate the WSN include Zigbee, Z-wave, INSTEON, Wavenis, and 6LoWPAN.

- **ZIGBEE** is one of the non-IP solutions that enable communication for intelligent objects. ZigBee is a wireless networking technology developed by the ZigBee Alliance for low-data rate and short-range applications (ZigBee Alliance, 2007). The ZigBee protocol stack is composed of four main layers: the physical (PHY) layer, the medium access control (MAC) layer, the network (NWK) layer, and the application (APL) layer. PHY and MAC of ZigBee are defined by the IEEE 802.15.4 standard, while the rest of the stack is defined by the ZigBee specification (Mainetti et al., 2011).
- **Z-WAVE** is another non-IP solution. Z-Wave is a wireless protocol architecture developed by ZenSys and promoted by the Z-Wave Alliance for automation in residential and light commercial environments. The primary purpose of Z-Wave is to allow reliable transmission of short messages from a control unit to one or more nodes in the network (Z-Wave, 2007).
- **INSTEON** is a solution developed for home automation by SmartLabs and promoted by the INSTEON Alliance. One of the distinctive features of INSTEON is the fact that it defines a mesh topology composed of RF and power line links. As a result, devices can be RF-only or power-line only or support both types of communication (Darbee, 2005).
- **Wavenis** is a wireless protocol stack developed by Coronis Systems for control and monitoring applications in several environments, including home and building automation. Wavenis is currently being promoted and managed by the Waves Open Standard Alliance (Wavenis-OSA). It defines the functionality of physical, link, and network layers (Garcia-Hernando et al., 2008).

Apart from the non-IP solutions, the industry has access to novel IP-enabled solutions to connect intelligent WSNs to the Ethernet network. IPv6 powers those solutions to create LowPower Wireless Personal Area Networks. The solution is called 6LoWPAN. The ideal use of 6LoWPAN is with applications where embedded devices need to communicate with Internet-based services using open standards to scale across large network infrastructures with mobility (Mainetti et al., 2011). In addition, other solutions, including Bluetooth smart, Constrained Application Protocol (CoAP), exist and are being used to enable different objects to be connected to the network for the industrial Internet (Shelby et al., 2011).

The wave of novel solutions gave birth to the proliferation of new and potential products that telecom companies could seize. New devices enabled by these protocols coupled with the arrival of IPv6 and IPv6-enabled smart devices could skyrocket the number of connected devices which need upgraded infrastructure. To cater to the new customers' needs—the owners of the new devices, telecoms need to innovate novel products and services. As an example of IoT application market and related innovative products, Al-Fukaha et al. (2015) state that healthcare applications and related IoT-based services such as mobile health (m-Health) and telecare that enable medical wellness, prevention, diagnosis, treatment, and monitoring services to be delivered efficiently through electronic media are expected to create about $1.1–$2.5 trillion in growth annually by the global economy by 2025. This wave of new devices and protocols comes with its challenges, mainly for the security and privacy of the data. The fifth generation of the 5G technology that is being developed pushes numerous devices online, but the lack of common standards in the industry hinders the early development of new products and services.

Widespread wireless connectivity also impacts Telecom's BMs regarding their market scope. First, let's look at the objects connected to the Internet. It is estimated that there are about 1.5 billion Internet-enabled PCs and over 1 billion Internet-enabled mobile phones today (Perera et al., 2015). These two categories are joined by Internet-enabled smart objects (Kortuem et al., 2010; Atzori et al., 2014.) in the future, and this has started to happen. By 2020, 50 to 100 billion devices will be connected to the Internet, ranging from smartphones, PCs, and ATMs (Automated Teller Machine) to manufacturing equipment in factories and products in shipping containers (Perera et al., 2014). Vermesan and Friess (2014, p. 26) argue that these new developments have the potential to transform products, channels, and company BMs radically. These new developments create disruptions in the business and opportunities for all types of organizations—OEMs, technology suppliers, system integrators, and global consultancies. There may be the opportunity to overturn established BMs, answer customer pain points, and grow the market in segments that cannot be served economically with today's offerings. In addition, the possibilities of widespread wireless connectivity enable the development of new customer bases from untapped segments of the market to date.

Examples of the application market for IoT enabled by wireless connectivity include smart cities (Caragliu et al., 2009). The concept of Smart Cities encompasses various innovative domains. Previous authors agree that intelligent transportation, smart security, and intelligent energy management are critical components for building smart cities (Zanella et al., 2014). Briefly, the IoT market scope cut across all the "smart" landscapes. Smart is the new green as defined by Frost and Sullivan (Frost and Sullivan, n.d.), and the green products and services are replaced by intelligent products and services (Vermesan et al., 2011). Frost and Sullivan (n.d.) add that smart cities be measured on the level of intelligence and integration of infrastructure that connects the healthcare, energy, building, transportation, and governance sectors. Therefore, the primary objectives for IoT are the creation of intelligent environments/spaces and self-aware things (e.g., intelligent transport, products, cities, buildings, rural areas, energy, health, and living) for climate, food, energy, mobility, digital society and health applications (Vermesan et al., 2011).

The rapid expansion of IoT enabled by widespread wireless connectivity reshuffles Telecom's BMs to include a broader market scope to contain the upcoming disruptive competition. In the EY's report entitled Digital Transformation for 2020 and Beyond (EY, 2017), 74% of their survey participants, high-ranking telecom executives, highlighted the disruptive competition as the top strategic challenge facing their businesses. Again, survey participants were asked to name their top three strategic priorities through 2020; three focus areas were cited by more than half of respondents: digital BMs (71%), customer experience (61%), and cost control and business efficiencies (53%) (EY, 2017). These findings show how urgent the Telecoms need to embrace IoT and digital BMs that widen their market scope (and product scope) to contain the competitive intensity of peripheral

TABLE 4.2
The Operator Views on Challenges Facing the Telecom Industry

1	Disruptive competition tops the list of industry challenges	5	Confidence is rising in the digital services opportunity, yet caveats remain.
2	Digital business models, customer experience, and cost control lead the 2020 strategic agenda.	6	Analytics and virtualization are the top innovation drivers, but legacy IT and a lack of skills are acting as brakes.
3	The network dominates the near-term spending agenda, but a range or IT improvements are also being sought.	7	Process automation leads the list of long-term IT enablers.
4	Network capex is trending up but IT spending profiles vary.	8	The post-200 landscape will be transformed by 5G.

Source: Adapted of EY (2017). Digital Transformation for 2020 and Beyond: A Global Telecommunications Study report.

industries. Furthermore, the same EY report (2017) says that OTT players such as WhatsApp, Facebook, and WeChat have redefined the customer experience in messaging and video services, luring traffic away from Telecom offerings such as SMS. These trends are playing out against a market background in which consumers and enterprises increasingly see value in multiservice packages, with quad-play and cloud packages driving new opportunities in each segment, respectively. Table 4.2 summarizes the operator views on challenges facing the telecom industry.

With billions of devices/things connected to the network and owners scattered around the world, plus the inevitable cloud service business and outsourcing model, IoT brings a new dimension of cross-border business aspect that needs to be dealt with in the BMs. Regulation and standardization play a paramount role in this regard. However, with most of the IoT standardization work still in the pipeline, time-to-market constraints are accelerating the deployment of a variety of fragmented and proprietary IoT products; there is still a lack of understanding of what an IoT service is meant to be, what its consequences are, and how to promote standard IoT services. In addition, there are significant gaps between legislative mechanisms concerning privacy between many countries such as Europe, Canada, and the USA (Meddeb, 2016).

Further, while there are claims about the need for common IoT standards, there is an overwhelming number of standards for IoT, emanating from mainstream standards development organizations (SDOs), mainly IETF, ITU-T, IEEE, ETSI, ISO/IEC, and the International Society of Automation (ISA), as well as other state-funded and international projects (Hoebeke et al., 2012). Therefore, without unified effort, instead of converging toward common standards, this overwhelming number of proposals might further exacerbate the confusion about services and regulation (Meddeb, 2016). We believe that digital BMs should consider this aspect. Lack of common standards hinders mass development of IoT products and services, but, according to the efforts deployed in this regard by multiple bodies worldwide, the hopes are high for the development of harmonized standards shortly. The lack of that common framework would make it harder for an American IoT product to be commercialized in Europe, China, and vice versa. Telecom companies' products depend on common international standards. A Canadian IoT product cannot cross the border into the USA if there are no common standards for that product to work on networks on both sides of the border. Digital BMs should reflect this reality.

Regarding the IoT service regulation, Meddeb (2016) points out that, while regulation of the traditional Internet is primarily driven by service, regulation of IoT is primarily driven by trust, security, and privacy. However, it is essential to add that, so far, a large part of the Internet community is opposing Internet regulation. The Internet Society (internetsociety.org) ensures that three critical aspects of the Internet are retained: *permission-less innovation, open access*, and *collaboration*.

IoT regulation aims to protect consumers but also promotes businesses. That is why several technology companies are promoting the virtues of self-regulation when it comes to managing consumer data (Lovrek et al., 2014). They further stress the benefits of leveraging large amounts of big data to simplify daily tasks and give consumers the option to make conscious decisions. Summing up his work, Meddeb (2016) concludes that the goal of a standard is typically to unify interfaces, protocols, and services so that various systems can be interconnected but also asks a crucial question: Do we have a common and clear understanding of a standard IoT service? In his words, the answer is quite mitigated. In fact, to some extent, the overwhelming number of standards might have contributed to further exacerbating the ambiguity about service and may deepen the interoperability issues. The overwhelming number of standards limits their scope to specific domains (M2M, WSN, and RFID) and stakeholders yielding isolated and redundant solutions.

Competence-wise, the IoT products and services for Telecom companies require adjustments. For example, we have started to deploy some products/services in intelligent buildings, smart grids, smart transportation, factory 4.0, and many more. Therefore, for a given company to deliver in all or most areas, its BMs need to opt for either open architecture or closed one. Furthermore, considering the rapidly increasing requirement of new knowledge and skills for the IoT products and services coupled with the volume of work that needs to be done, companies need to outsource part of the competencies they do not have in-house.

When asked about the most significant barriers to their organization's digital transformation journey, 65% of the Telecom executives surveyed by EY (2017) responded that IT legacy platform and architecture burden took the first place. The architecture should be flexible enough to accommodate the needs of rapid product development and deployment. Fleisch (2007) pointed out that if IoT would like to follow the successful path of the classical Internet, its architecture would have to make sure that any computer could, in principle, access any tagged object. For that matter, a global standard protocol, identification, and addressing scheme for bridging the last mile from the Internet to the innovative things would be required. He added that, in an ideal open IoT architecture, not only can every sensor be reached by every authorized computer or person, but in addition, every person and organization can set up their services, link them with identifiers, and offer them to the public.

In this regard, Khan et al. (2012) suggest that the proposed architecture for IoT needs to address many factors like scalability, interoperability, reliability, and QoS. Moreover, since IoT connects peer-to-peer to exchange information among themselves, the traffic and storages in the network also increase exponentially.

The availability of multiple protocols, IP-based and non-IP-based solutions to the connectivity of objects is a positive development in the IoT era, and an obstacle since harmonization has been very slow, causing interoperability issues worldwide.

4.5.2 Microcontrollers

The second key IoT technological driver that affects the Telecoms' BMs is the availability of low-cost and powerful microcontrollers. Microcontrollers (MCUs), the tiny sensors that enable connectivity and control in all the "Things" around us, have now become so inexpensive—at around $1 a piece—that they can be incorporated in just about everything, from industrial machinery and home appliances to wearable devices and even clothing (Morgan Stanley, 2016).

4.5.3 Decreasing Cost of Megabit/Sec

On top of that, Investment and upgrades in infrastructure like fiber optic and the economies of scale and economies of scope have pushed the cost of high-speed Internet downward in terms of the megabit per second data transfer rate unit. High-speed Internet is central to the implementation of IoT solutions. With the decreasing cost of broadband Internet, the deployment of IoT solutions looks much more accessible. With 50 billion devices connected to the Internet by 2020 according to Cisco (2011) and with all data (big data) they generate that need to be uploaded and downloaded for different reasons, including analytics and storage/archive, having the networks to support all of our devices be crucial to the success of IoT overall (Colt, 2014). IDC forecasts that, by 2020, the number of connected devices will grow to 32 billion and comprise 10% of the world's data. The world's data will amount to 44 zettabytes by 2020, 10% of it from IoT (Adshead, 2014). Compounding the challenge, IoT devices generate data constantly, and often analysis must be very rapid. For example, when the temperature in a chemical vat is fast approaching the acceptable limit, corrective action must be taken almost immediately. In the time it takes for temperature readings to travel from the edge to the cloud for analysis, the opportunity to avert a lousy batch might be lost (Cisco, 2015). This statement highlights the importance of high-speed Internet to enable IoT deployment.

4.5.4 Decreasing Cost of CPU, Memory, and Storage

Among the key technological drivers of IoT, there is also the decreasing cost of CPU, memory, and storage. The projected growing number of connected devices generates zettabytes of data. Those data need substantial storage facilities, system memory, and high CPU capacity. Low costs associated with these three items only propel the implementation of IoT solutions. According to Adegbija et al. (2018), computing on IoT devices introduces new substantial challenges since IoT devices' microprocessors must satisfy increasingly growing computational and memory demands, maintain connectivity and adhere to stringent design and operational constraints, such as low cost, low energy budgets, and in some cases, real-time constraints. Data centers and cloud systems are part of the solutions to the fast-growing amount of data generated by IoT, but these must be affordable to consumers to continue rolling out IoT solutions. On top of providing data center facilities, the falling prices of data storage are one of the catalysts for IoT adoption down the line. Telecoms have to be more efficient and cost-effective than many third-party including Microsoft, IBM, Amazon, and GE (The Economist Intelligent Unit, 2013), that already offer (cloud) storage services to businesses. Fortunately, cloud computing and storage pricing demonstrates the ongoing reduction in storage costs—the price of storing a gigabyte of data on a public cloud service fell from 25 cents in 2010 to .024 cents by late 2014 (The Economist Intelligence Unit, 2017). Teu (2014) signaled that the cloud storage war being waged by Amazon, Google, and Microsoft has been well publicized and results in the cost of all cloud infrastructure, including storage racing to zero.

4.5.5 Sensors and Actuators Advances

Many factors have propelled the widespread rollout of IoT solutions. The availability of cheap and efficient sensors for every need (anything that can be sensed) is one. In addition, recent technological advances in low power integrated circuits and wireless communications have made available efficient, low cost, low power miniature devices for use in remote sensing applications. Combining these factors has improved the viability of utilizing a sensor network consisting of many intelligent sensors, enabling collecting, processing, analyzing, and disseminating valuable information gathered in various environments (Gubbi, 2013). IoT and connected sensors drive human well-being improvements in healthcare, water, agriculture, natural resource management, resiliency to climate change, and energy (ITU, 2016). Today, sensors are found in many everyday devices. Some of the latest smartphones come with at least ten embedded sensors, for example, a microphone to capture sounds, camera(s) to capture images (front and back), a fingerprint sensor, a global positioning system (GPS), accelerometer, gyroscope, thermometer, pedometer, heart rate monitor, light sensor, touch screen, and barometer (not to mention the various connectivity technologies such as Wi-Fi, Bluetooth, GSM/CDMA, LTE, and NFC) (Nick, 2014). The advances in embedded sensors, processing, and wireless connectivity are bringing the power of the digital world to objects and places in the physical world (Vermesan and Friess, 2014). Ericsson and Cisco predicted that 50 billion small embedded sensors and actuators be connected to the Internet by 2020 (Cisco, 2015; ITU, 2016).

Different researches have praised the role of sensors in enabling future networks. For example, in the study made by the European Parliament's Directorate-General for Internal Policies (2015) entitled "Over-the-counter (OTTs) players: Market dynamics and policy challenges," they found out that the high cost of labor, energy, fuel, and infrastructure makes automation and optimization enabled by sensors and connectivity an intelligent investment for many businesses and smart industry in many European countries. For widespread adoption of IoT, the cost of basic hardware must continue to drop. Low-cost, low-power sensors are essential, and the price of MEMS (micro-electromechanical systems) sensors, which are used in smartphones, has dropped by 30 to 70% in the past five years (McKinsey Global Institute, 2015).

4.5.6 IPv6 and 5G

Sensors need the power to work for a long time autonomously. Because of their large number, they also need a good network to transmit the large amount of data they generate. Different standards and protocols have been developed that make them use low power and operate for the longest time possible. Protocols for the Wireless Sensor Network (WSN) and the ability of the object to connect to the Internet are being developed and used. Also, IPv4, as we know it today with a limited range of possible IP addresses that can be assigned to different nodes on the network, would not sustain the projected billions of objects connected to the IoT network worldwide. The advent of IPv6 solves this situation and boosts IoT solutions implementation. The global deployment of IPv6 worldwide enables global and ubiquitous addressing of any communicating intelligent things. The current transition of the global Internet to IPv6 provides a virtually unlimited number of public IP addresses able to provide bidirectional and symmetric (true M2M) access to billions of bright things. It paves the way to new IoT interconnection and integration (Vermesan and Friess, 2014). These authors reiterate that IPv6 provides a large-scale addressing scheme and a native integration with the worldwide Internet and a source of many relevant and valuable features, including self-configuration mechanisms and secure end-to-end connections.

With IPv4 exhaustion back in 2011 (Richter et al., 2015), IoT development was likely impacted due to the high number of IP addresses needed to connect billions of objects to the network. On the contrary, IPv6 makes the new conception of extending the Internet to consumer devices, physical systems, and any imaginable thing that can benefit from the connectivity. IPv6 spreads the addressing space to support all the emerging Internet-enabled devices. In addition, IPv6 has been designed to provide secure communications to users and mobility for all devices attached to the user; thereby, users can always be connected (Vermesan and Friess, 2014). In parallel to IPv6, several IPv6-related standards have emerged, including, among others, the IPv6 over Low Power WPAN (6LoWPAN), providing a lighter version of IPv6 for constrained nodes and networks (Kushalnagar et al., 2007).

Multiple objects in IoT need to be seamlessly connected to the network. The 5G of the wireless network provided a solution to that question. 5G may be a timely technology offering lower cost, lower energy consumption, and support for many devices. 5G puts together and integrates a heterogeneous set of wireless access technologies, enabling seamless connectivity, said Palattella et al. (2016), who also concludes that, once market demand for IoT services is created, 5G constitutes an essential enabler of a complete IoT rollout. According to Vermesan and Friess (2014), 5G networks deliver 1,000 to 5,000 times more capacity than 3G and 4G networks today and are cells that support peak rates of between 10 and 100 Gbps. West (2016) suggested that this new era of 5G brings together improved connectivity, cloud-based storage, and an array of connected devices and services. Extensive computing capability combined with virtual system architecture opens up a mobile IoT.

4.5.7 Cloud Computing, Big Data, and Analytics

Businesses adopt IoT because they need valuable data it generates. Many sensors produce a large volume of data in an unstructured format that needs to be quickly and efficiently analyzed to give decision-makers timely insights. Without adequate analytical tools and knowledge, IoT is nothing, and it would not attract users. McKinsey Global Institute (2015) mentioned some examples of the importance of big data analytics. In one case study from the Canadian tar sands, advanced analytics raised daily production by 5 to 8% by allowing managers to schedule and allocate staff and equipment more effectively. In another example, when Rio Tinto's crews prepare a new site for blasting, they collect information on the geological formation where they are working. Operations managers can provide blasting crews with detailed information to calibrate their use of explosives better, allowing them to adjust for the characteristics of the ore in different parts of the pit. Without real-time data about the quality of the ore and the status and availability of equipment, such optimization would not have been possible, and the company would have had to rely on cruder methods, such as using correlations between productivity and number of employees per activity to allocate resources. In the Internet of Things Business Index 2017 of The Economist's Intelligence Unit (2017), when asked which organizational capabilities are considered to be most important to IoT success, 45% of surveyed business executives said technology innovation and 32% say data analytics, while 25% cite BM innovation as a success factor. ABI Research suggests that IoT hardware and connectivity revenues grow at 10–20% annually, while apps, analytics, and services grow at 40–50% annually (ITU, 2016). In contrast, Gartner estimates that IoT product and service suppliers could generate incremental revenue over US$300 billion by 2020, resulting in US$1.9 trillion in global economic added value (Gartner, 2013), while IDC forecasts that the worldwide market for IoT solutions grows from US$1.9 trillion in 2013 to US$7.1 trillion in 2020 (ITU, 2016).

TABLE 4.3
Strategic Scope of IoT

Key Technological Drivers	Product Scope	Market Scope	Geographical Scope	Scope of Competencies
Widespread Wireless connectivity: Improved and reliable connectivity technologies and protocols ZigBee, Z-Wave, Bluetooth Smart, Wi-Fi, etc.	1. Innovating offerings for new smart devices 2. IPv6 and a huge number of connected devices need infrastructure upgrade to cater for new products/services 3. Security and privacy challenge 4. 5 G Infrastructure 5. Lack of common standards	1. Widening market limits to take advantage of new IoT opportunities 2. Meeting needs of New types of customers 3. Disruptive competition 4. Changing customer needs and attitudes	1. IoT Standards harmonization (European Vs American Vs international standards) 2. Regulations impact on the IoT business and cross-border business aspect	1. Open architecture will allow for collaboration and co-creation of value in the industry as opposed to a closed one

Microcontrollers:
Availability of low cost and powerful microcontrollers, these power the sensor nodes (mote).

1. Traffic explosion due to a higher number of nodes
2. Device certification, activation and ordering

1. Shortening time-to-market for new products and services
2. A growing number of new types of service demands
3. Catering to the new market of "smart things"

1. New customers localized in remote areas like farmers, fishermen, drivers, and even international making more Telecoms go international

1. Open architecture eases interoperability

Decreasing cost of megabit/second

1. OTTs growing their share of industry value chain revenues (10%)
2. Integrated different solutions for different things into one platform—Interoperability

1. More customers using remote services, implying cloud computing
2. Competition between retail and distribution providers

1. Managed service provision (MSP) needs

(Continued)

TABLE 4.3 (*Continued*)

Key Technological Drivers	Product Scope	Market Scope	Geographical Scope	Scope of Competencies
Decreasing cost of CPU, memory, & storage	1. Data centers and cloud infrastructure to cater to the increasing need for storage space 2. Platform-as-service	1. Small businesses affording to stock their data	1. With cloud-based services, it is more likely that Telecoms will have more out-of-the-country customers	
Sensors and actuators advancement: Availability of cheap and efficient sensors for every need (anything that can be sensed)	1. Co-creation of innovative products 2. Partnering with platform providers 3. Digitizing the physical world through sensors and connected devices.	1. New application markets such as smart cities, smart manufacturing, wearables, smart grid, smart transportation… 2. Selective business models and flexible partnerships to the fore	1. Novel offerings beyond traditional geographic limits of Telecoms 2. Global supply chain and logistics	1. Leveraging learnings from other industries 2. Open architecture for interoperability and co-creation

IPv6 and 5G	1. Infrastructure-as-service	1. High demand for smart things opens possibilities for a novel market	1. Open architecture allows every player to deploy IPv6 and 5G-based products	1. Skills upgrade for engineers needed
Cloud computing, Big data, and analytics: possibility to analyze the huge chunk of data gathered by IoT devices and make some sense out of it and use it for decision making	1. Smart applications for smart things 2. Software-as-service	1. Predictive and prescriptive analytics 2. Infrastructure-as-a-service	1. Cloud platforms shared by geographically dispersed customers 2. Satisfying need/support of remote/international/global customers	1. New Skilled professionals and new skill sets 2. Outsourcing is inevitable 3. Data monetization is key 4. Lack of senior management knowledge/commitment 5. Ned for data scientists and data analysts

Cloud computing enables a large amount of data to be stored and accessed anytime from anywhere on multiple devices. Many companies have invested in the infrastructure and opened it to the public for data storage. With the falling storage prices, companies can deploy many devices without worrying about the cost of data storage space. The development of cloud storage is an essential resource in this respect, owing to its wide availability and scalability, said The Economist's Intelligence Unit in its IoT Business Index 2017. Today, many third parties, including Amazon and GE, provide cloud services for managing big data, they added, arguing that IoT is an idea whose time has finally come. Falling technology costs, developments in complementary fields like mobile and cloud, together with support from governments, have all contributed to the dawning of an IoT "quiet revolution." On this note, Gubbi et al. (2013) added that cloud computing could provide the virtual infrastructure for such utility computing, which integrates monitoring devices, storage devices, analytics tools, visualization platforms, and client delivery. The cost-based model that Cloud computing offers enables end-to-end service provisioning for businesses and users to access applications on demand from anywhere.

The data swamps resulting from the growing number of connected objects on the network are worth money. Data monetization made possible by advanced data analytics is an essential element in the IoT-centered BMs. For Telecoms to capture this revenue stream, they need to consider including this in their strategies. Creating new products and services based on big data helped companies capture revenue from non-traditional communication companies. More importantly, for companies to do so, they need new personnel with new skill sets like data analysts and data scientists. With companies adding on new functions and areas of business because of the IoT rollout, outsourcing non-core functions helps companies be more focused and agile, delivering services to more demanding customers.

The strategic scope of IoT for product scope, market scope, geographical scope, and scope of competencies can be summarized in Table 4.3.

Chapter 5

A CASE STUDY

Bell Canada Enterprises (BCE) Inc.

This chapter highlights the results of our research into the IoT business models in the Telecom industry with a case study of BCE Inc.

5.1 METHODOLOGY

We analyzed one Telecom company, BCE Inc., and came up with several IoT-based products/services that explain where they are in their journey of deploying this technology. We chose to work with BCE Inc. because it is one of the biggest Telecom companies in Canada, operates from coast to coast, and has one of the most extensive infrastructures in the country. In addition, we believe that Bell is representative of Telecom companies that have the means (infrastructure, financial, and expertise) to roll out any new technology.

To demonstrate what we talked about in Chapters 1 and 2 about our objectives and using the methodology above, we dived into BCE annual reports (2017 and 2018), website, press releases, white papers, and other resources to come up with some examples of their IoT products and services per primary application market. The study of those documents and other sources of information resulted in ten broad categories of IoT business models, as shown below. At the same time, this exercise helped us highlight some of the company's difficulties in implementing this technology.

5.2 BCE Inc. DESCRIPTION

BCE Inc. is a holding company for Bell Canada and Bell Media. Bell Canada comprises many companies, including Bell Mobility, Bell Aliant, Virgin Mobile, Lucky Mobile, Bell T.V. and Bell Fibre Tv, and many more, whereas Belly Media comprises different media channels

DOI: 10.1201/9781003294412-5

like CTV Television Network and CP24 Toronto. The information provided in this section falls under the Bell Canada subsidiary.

BCE Inc. was born in 1983 when Bell Canada, Northern Telcom became subsidiaries of BCE Inc. and many other small companies through corporate reorganization. BCE Inc. is a publicly traded telecommunications holding and is one of the biggest in Canada in terms of revenue and capitalization.

Like many other Telcom companies, Bell has included IoT in its strategic imperatives by leveraging its existing broadband and wireless infrastructure. Their motive is that

> greater customer adoption of data services, including mobile T.V., international data roaming, mobile commerce, and mobile banking, as well as other IoT applications in the areas of retail (e.g., home automation), business (e.g., remote monitoring), transportation (e.g., connected car and asset tracking) and urban city optimization (smart cities), is expected to accelerate growth opportunities as well as competition in these areas.
>
> (BCE Inc. Annual Report, 2018)

5.3 THE CASE OF BCE

After all the sources of information were analyzed, we came up with ten different categories of IoT business models. Again, these business models highlight that traditional Telecoms can build and rely on the existing broadband fiber and mobile connectivity infrastructure to deliver IoT solutions. However, the results show that the same companies need to make acquisitions and partnerships with other solution providers to be more competitive to shorten the "time-to-market" factor. These new acquisitions and partnerships provide invaluable technologies and intelligent devices that Telecoms do not necessarily have in-house.

Our findings are summarized in Table 5.1 highlighting some IoT business models at BCE Inc.

Table 5.1 gives BCE's main business models based on IoT technology as of the fiscal year ending in 2018.

Table 5.1 gives examples of major BCE IoT-based business models. It reveals that BCE has built upon its existing infrastructure and services to deliver some IoT-based products and services in the areas of agriculture, global connectivity, logistics and transport, mobility, asset management, smart city, and energy management. It is also clear

TABLE 5.1

Major BCE's Market-Driven IoT-Based Business Models

Product Line / Application Market	Examples and Details
1 Smart City And Energy management	**Smart City** (City of Kingston and Bell partnered for a pioneer project plus Connected Homes and delivering bold new home and wireless services that take broadband further. Bell **partnered with Echologics to deliver an IoT Smart City** solution for the City of Medicine Hat in Alberta to wirelessly monitor the city's water pipeline network to help reduce water loss. **Bell is the exclusive Canadian carrier to offer GridPoint,** a data-driven energy management solution that enables you to optimize energy consumption and cut costs. GridPoint offers real-time visibility, monitoring, and control of energy usage across multiple sites. Bell is a partner in Smart City initiatives with the Ontario cities Kingston, Markham, Orillia, and St. Catharines; Medicine Hat, Alberta; Whitehorse, Yukon; and St. John's, Newfoundland and Labrador.
2 IoT platform	**LTE-M** (Long Term Evolution—Category M1) network supports the rapidly increasing use of IoT devices on low-power, wide-area networks (LPWANs) in Canada. **Bell IoT Starter Kit** (three Sims with Bell connectivity, 30 MB/SIM per month for three months, 50 SMS messages per Sim per month.
3 Mobility (Smart car)	Bell enabled built-in Wi-Fi hotspots in **Ford** and **Lincoln** vehicles with **Bell's Connected Car Built In service**, providing on-the-go connectivity for up to ten devices at a time and enabling data sharing across customer smartphone plans.
4 Remote monitoring	Superior Propane implemented Bell's national fuel tank monitoring solution for its business and residential customers.

(Continued)

TABLE 5.1 *(Continued)*

Product Line / Application Market	Examples and Details
5 Global connectivity	**Global SIM**: Access to 70+ carriers in over 120 countries.
6 Telematics	**Telematics** from Bell is a usage-based insurance solution that tracks critical data while vehicles are underway, including speed, braking, time traveled, and locations covered during each trip. **Bell partnered with Hyundai AutoEver Telematics America** (HATA) to provide multiple telematics, safety and security, and infotainment services for the latest Hyundai and Kia vehicles on the Bell network.
7 Wireless backup connectivity for IoT	**Bell's wireless backup solutions** keep businesses communicating even when the primary data connection is lost.
8 Digital signage	**Partnership with Convergent Media Systems and Sony of Canada Ltd.**: Bell's digital signage solution encompasses all ad content creation and in-store equipment, including digital screens for displaying the ads, as well as real-time reporting capabilities.
9 Agriculture	**Bell Partnered with BeWhere Technologies and Huawei** to implement an automated IoT solution for the Henry of Pelham Vineyard. As a result, the winery can monitor temperature and water levels, prevent vine diseases, improve plant health, lower operating costs, and provide years of maintenance-free data gathering by using environmental wireless sensors connected to the Bell LTE-M wireless network. Bell MTS Inc. launched the **Innovations in Agriculture Program** at the University of Manitoba, providing students with opportunities to develop innovative IoT Technologies for agriculture and food science application.

(Continued)

TABLE 5.1 *(Continued)*

Product Line / Application Market	Examples and Details
10 Logistics and Transportation (Fleet management solutions)	In partnership with **BeWhere** and **Trak-iT**, Bell introduced **Fleet Freedom**, Canada's first integrated fleet management and asset tracking solution, delivered exclusively over Bell's LTE-M network. Fleet Freedom gives remote access to a vehicle's current speed, engine idle state, location, address, heading, GPS odometer, and zone status. Run reports on-demand and set up an automated schedule for an entire company or select vehicles. **Asset Management** in real-time is a solution that lets users effectively manage their machinery and fleet—without a significant investment of capital or labor.
11 Manufacturing	**Bell teamed with Icicle Technologies to provide food manufacturers** across the country with a remote tracking and monitoring solution to enhance food safety.

that some of these products/services can be trans-boundaries like the Global SIM that gives users access to more than 70 carriers in over 120 countries worldwide. These examples show that it is possible to roll out IoT-based projects, but the scale is still small. They also imply difficulties that old players have encountered in adopting IoT as a significant source of revenue. Compared to the size, infrastructure, experience of the company, IoT products/solutions are not yet visible to the general public and are far from becoming a significant source of income. Again, the annual reports (2017 and 2018) do not show part of the revenue attributable to the IoT sector. This lack of information might imply that it is too early for the company to gain enough from IoT to be highlighted in the reports.

While Telecoms like Bell Canada and others are yet to gain from IoT, non-traditional players have gained ground and threatening old players. The continued OTT-based substitution and market expansion of lower-cost VoIP and software-defined networking in a vast area network (SD-WAN) solutions, which are attracting global competitors, including traditional software players, are changing the approach to service offers and pricing and could hurt their business, says the annual report (2018). The same report goes on to mention that

> As the scope of our businesses increases and evolving technologies drive new services, delivery models and strategic partnerships, our competitive landscape intensifies and expands to include new and emerging competitors, certain of which were historically our partners or suppliers, as well as global-scale competitors including, in particular, OTT TV service providers, IoT hardware and software providers, voice over I.P. (VoIP) providers and other web-based and OTT players that are penetrating the telecommunications space with significant resources and a large customer base to amortize costs. Certain of these competitors are changing the competitive landscape by moving beyond being mere disruptors and newer entrants to the industry to establishing material positions.
>
> (BCE Inc. Annual Report, 2018)

In comparison to Qingjun's (2018) model, a clear relationship is visible regarding the recommended business models for Telecom operators. IoT platform, connectivity, and general-purpose industry suites are the main B.M. seen at BCE Inc. For example, the LTE-M and Bell IoT Starter Kit are IoT platforms compared to the recommended Model 3 by Qingjun (2018); the Fleet Freedom and Asset Management fall under the Model 5 as business suites that customers can deploy and customize to suit their business needs. In addition, smart city solutions can also fall under this category to some extent. Overall, the main IoT-based BMs tend to build, in general, on the existing infrastructure that the company has been using for years.

Chapter 6 provides the conclusion and highlights some recommendations to the Telecom operators.

IoT AND THE FUTURE OF THE TELECOM INDUSTRY

The objective of this book is to highlight the IoT-based business models in the Telecom industry in the first place, and in the second place to assess the impact of IoT on the telecom industry's revenue streams and to carry out a PESTLE analysis of the industry about IoT as well as identify key IoT technological drivers. First, we reviewed the main IoT business models in the literature review. Then, through a case study of BCE Inc., we identified ten key IoT Business models that the company is, by partnerships with other companies or through acquisitions, implementing as per available information. The information that is not available is the revenue streams from these projects, suggesting that the company might not have started gaining from IoT business models yet. However, the findings show that the company is leveraging its existing broadband fiber and mobile connectivity infrastructure to roll out some IoT-based projects. One of the biggest revelations is that despite BCE Inc. is one of the biggest Telecom companies in the industry, it is far from self-sufficient in rolling out this kind of technology. Hence partnerships or acquisitions are needed. The reason might be that the technology is still early, and no companies have mastered it as its most skills are still not developed at their best.

The impact of IoT on the telecoms' revenue streams revealed that new entrants who are not necessarily in the telecom industry have been able to roll out some IoT products and services that impact the old players' revenue streams. OTT services are the biggest culprit. Services like YouTube, WhatsApp, IPTV, and Netflix have gained a significant market share that was formerly part and parcel of the telecoms' revenue streams. On this note, BCE Inc.'s annual report (2018) recognizes that if the company does not step up the development of IoT business models, there is a considerable risk of losing a market share and revenues to non-conventional telecom operators namely OTTs.

In this book, seven enablers have been identified as the key technological drivers to IoT advancement. These enablers include the widespread wireless connectivity, the availability and affordability of microcontrollers, sensors, and actuators, the decreasing cost of bandwidth, the recent implementation of IPv6, and the ongoing development of the 5G network use cloud computing and analytics. Altogether, these factors continue to be at the helm of IoT advancement. It is believed that once 5G is fully operational, more objects become connected, thanks to the capacity of this cellular mobile communication in terms of energy saving, high data rate, and tremendous cost reduction. In addition, thanks to IPV6, I.P. addresses are more available than ever to be used on a large number of connected objects. These factors, coupled with more R&D and investment, propel the IoT rollout.

The PESTLE analysis revealed that several factors still impede the IoT implementation even though other factors favor its development. The lack of a comprehensive political and regulatory framework still slows down IoT deployment, among other factors. The multitude of protocols spread around the world also hinder the interoperability of systems, which is of prime importance to the world-level advancement of technology. Other factors such as security of data and systems, privacy and acceptability among the general public, and lack of skills are also on the list of constraints. On the other hand, though, general economic conditions in most developed and developing economies are favorable to the advancement of IoT technology. These general economic conditions witness governments willing to subsidize R&D in this field and have partnered with the private sector (mainly telecom operators, universities, and regulatory organizations) to speed up the rollout process. In addition, many governments have put money into the smart city, smart mobility, intelligent energy, industry 4.0, and many more initiatives with the hope to benefit the general public in terms of public health and environmental protection.

From our findings, for telecom companies to take advantage of the fast-developing IoT technology, three things are essential and should be kept at the center of all IoT initiatives. To start with, they need to revisit their business models and services or build brand new ones compatible with IoT. These three things enable Telecoms to create new market opportunities and revenue streams. On top of this, Telecoms can enhance the customer experience. Therefore, if telecom operators want to succeed in digital transformation, they need to utilize IoT technology. For IoT inclusion in telecom business models, based on the findings in BCE Inc.'s case study, we back the model suggested by Qingjun (2018), who says that traditional models of network construction, service rollout, and selling data traffic cannot be applied to developing IoT services and suggests to reconstruct their business models. Telecoms can capitalize on their infrastructure by adding enhancements to accommodate IoT systems. Good redesigns and investments in R&D would allow the industry to achieve this goal. Monetizing data from IoT-enabled objects and better cloud infrastructure, partnering with others to create a complete IoT ecosystem continue to play an essential role in the industry going forward. IoT should be central to all telecom operators that want to keep playing in the ever-changing industry that faces many challenges borne out of the current digital transformation of everything.

APPLICATION MARKETS FOR IoT

	Application Markets	Examples
1	**Cities**	
1.1	Smart Parking	Monitoring of parking spaces available in the city
1.2	Structural health	Monitoring of vibrations and material conditions in buildings, bridges, and historical monuments
1.3	Noise Urban Maps	Sound monitoring in bar areas and centric zones in real time
1.4	Traffic Congestion	Monitoring of vehicles and pedestrian levels to optimize driving and walking routes
1.5	Smart Lighting	Intelligent and weather adaptive lighting in streetlights
1.6	Waste Management	Detection of rubbish levels in containers to optimize the trash collection routes
1.7	Intelligent Transportation Systems	Intelligent Roads and Intelligent Highways with warning messages and diversions according to climate conditions and unexpected events like accidents or traffic jams

(*Continued*)

(*Continued*)

	Application Markets	Examples
2	**Environment**	
2.1	Forest Fire Detection	Monitoring of combustion gases and preemptive fire conditions to define alert zones
2.2	Air pollution	Control of CO_2 emissions of factories, pollution emitted by cars, and toxic gases generated in farms
2.3	Landslide and Avalanche Prevention	Monitoring of soil moisture, vibrations, and earth density to detect dangerous patterns in land conditions
2.4	Earthquake Early Detection	Distributed control in specific places of tremors
3	**Water**	
3.1	Water quality	Study of water suitability in rivers and the sea for fauna and eligibility for drinkable use
3.2	Water Leakages	Detection of a liquid presence outside tanks and pressure variations along pipes
3.3	River Floods	Monitoring of water level variations in rivers, dams, and reservoirs
4	**Energy Smart Grid, Smart Metering**	
4.1	Smart grid	Energy consumption monitoring and management
4.2	Tank level	Monitoring of water, oil, and gas levels in storage tanks and cisterns
4.3	Photovoltaic Installations	Monitoring and optimization of performance in solar energy plants
4.4	Water flow	Measurement of water pressure in water transportation systems
4.5	Silos Stock Calculation	Measurement of emptiness level and weight of the goods
5	**Security & Emergencies**	
5.1	Perimeter Access Control	Access control to restricted areas and detection of people in non-authorized areas

(*Continued*)

(*Continued*)

	Application Markets	Examples
5.2	Liquid Presence	Liquid detection in data centers, warehouses, and sensitive building grounds to prevent breakdowns and corrosions
5.3	Radiation Levels	Distributed measurement of radiation levels in nuclear power stations surroundings to generate leakage alerts
5.4	Explosive and Hazardous Gases	Detection of gas levels and leakages in industrial environments, surroundings of chemical factories, and inside mines
6	**Retail**	
6.1	Supply Chain Control	Monitoring of storage conditions along the supply chain and product tracking for traceability purposes
6.2	NFC Payment	Payment processing based on location or activity duration for public transport, gyms, and theme parks
6.3	Intelligent Shopping Applications	Getting advice at the point of sale according to customers habits, preferences, presence of allergic components for them, or expiring dates
6.4	Smart Product Management	Control of rotation of products in shelves in warehouses to automate restocking processes
7	**Logistics**	
7.1	Quality of Shipment Conditions	Monitoring of vibrations, strokes, container openings, or cold chain maintenance for insurance purposes
7.2	Item Location	A search of individual items in big surfaces like warehouses or harbors
7.3	Storage Incompatibility Detection	Warning emission on containers storing inflammable goods close to others containing explosive material
7.4	Fleet tracking	Control of routes followed for delicate goods like medical drugs, jewels, or dangerous merchandises

(*Continued*)

(*Continued*)

Application Markets	Examples
8	**Industrial Control**
8.1	M2M Applications	Machine auto-diagnosis and asset controls
8.2	Indoor Air Quality	Monitoring of toxic gas and oxygen levels inside chemical plants to ensure workers and goods safety
8.3	Temperature Monitoring	Control of temperature inside industrial and medical fridges with sensitive merchandise
8.4	Ozone Presence	Monitoring of ozone levels during the drying meat process in food factories
8.5	Indoor Location	Asset indoor location by using active (ZigBee, UWB) and passive tags (RFID/NFC)
8.6	Vehicle Auto-diagnosis	Information collection from CAN Bus to send real-time alarms to emergencies or provide advice to drivers
9	**Agriculture**	
9.1	Wine Quality Enhancing	Wine Quality Enhancing: Monitoring soil moisture and trunk diameter in vineyards to control the amount of sugar in grapes and grapevine health
9.2	Green Houses	Control micro-climate conditions to maximize the production of fruits and vegetables and their quality
9.3	Golf Courses	Selective irrigation in dry zones to reduce the water resources required in the green
9.4	Meteorological Station Network	Study of weather conditions in the field to forecast ice formation, rain, drought, snow, or wind changes
9.5	Compost	Control of humidity and temperature levels in alfalfa, hay, and straw to prevent fungus and other microbial contaminants
10	**Animal Farming**	
10.1	Offspring Care	Control of growing conditions of the offspring in animal farms to ensure its survival and health

(*Continued*)

(Continued)

	Application Markets	Examples
10.2	Animal Tracking	Location and identification of animals grazing in open pastures or location in big stables
10.3	Toxic Gas Levels	Study of ventilation and air quality in farms and detection of harmful gases from excrements
11	**Domotic & Home Automation**	
11.1	Energy and Water Use	Energy and water supply consumption monitoring to obtain advice on how to save cost and resources
11.2	Remote Control Appliances	Switching on and off remotely appliances to avoid accidents and save energy
11.3	Intrusion Detections Systems	Detection of window and door openings and violations to prevent intruders
11.4	Art and Goods Preservation	Monitoring of conditions inside museums and art warehouses
12	**eHealth**	
12.1	Fall Detection	Assistance for elderly or disabled people living independently
12.2	Medical Fridges	Control of conditions inside freezers storing vaccines, medicines, and organic elements
12.3	Sportsmen Care	Vital signs monitoring in high-performance centers and fields
12.4	Patients Surveillance	Vital signs monitoring in high-performance centers and older adults' homes
12.5	Ultraviolet Radiation	Measurement of U.V. sun rays to warn people to avoid exposed during certain hours

Source: Adapted from Vermesan and Friess (2013) Internet of Things: Converging Technologies for Smart Environments and Integrated Ecosystems. P.32.

BIBLIOGRAPHY

Adegbija, T., Rogacs, A., Patel, C. and Gordon-Ross, A. (2018). Microprocessor optimizations for the internet of things: A survey. *IEEE Transactions on Computer-Aided Design of Integrated Circuits and Systems*, Vol. 37 No. 1, pp. 7–20, Jan. 2018.

Adshead, A. (2014). Data set to grow 10-fold by 2020 as the internet of things take off. Retrieved from http://www.computerweekly.com/news/2240217788/Data-set-to-grow-10-fold-by-2020-as-internet-of-things-takes-off, [Accessed on March 25, 2018].

Al-Fukaha, A., Guizi, M., Mohammadi, M., Aledhari, M. and Ayyash, M. (2015). Internet of things: A survey on enabling technologies, protocols, and applications. *IEEE Communication Surveys & Tutorials*, Vol. 17 No. 4, 4th Quarter 2015.

Ashton, K. (2009). *That "Internet of Things" Thing.* Retrieved from http://www.rfidjournal.com/articles/view?4986, [Accessed March 6, 2019].

Atzori, L., Iera, A. and Morabito, G. (2014). From 'smart objects' to 'social objects': The next evolutionary step of the Internet of Things. *IEEE Communication Magazine*, Vol. 52 No. 1, pp. 97–105.

Bandyopadhyay, D. and Sen, J. Internet of Things: applications and challenges in technology and standardization. *Wireless Personal Communications*, Vol. 58, pp. 49–69 (2011). 10.1007/s11277-011-0288-5.

Berthelsen, E. (2015). *A new agenda item for enterprise executives: Enterprise IoT.* Machina Research (white paper).

Bork, Robert H. Gregory Sidak, J. (2013). The misuse of profit margins to infer market power. *Journal of Competition Law & Economics*, Vol, 9 No. 3, September, pp. 511–530. 10.1093/joclec/nht024.

Brown, E. (2016). *Who Needs the Internet of Things?* Retrieved from https://www.linux.com/news/who-needs-internet-things, [Accessed March 10, 2019].

Bughin, Jacques, Chui, Michael and Manyika, James (2015). *An executive's guide to the Internet of Things*, McKinsey, August.

Caragliu, A., Bo, C.D. and Nijkamp, P. (2009). Smart Cities in Europe. In *Proceeding of 3rd Central European Conference Regional Science (CERS)*, pp. 45–59. Retrieved from https://inta-aivn.org/images/cc/Urbanism/background%20documents/01_03_Nijkamp.pdf, [Accessed on March 22, 2018].

Chesbrough, H. and Rosenbloom, R.-S. (2002). The role of business model in capturing value from innovation: Evidence from Xerox Corporation's technology spinoff companies. *Harvard Business School*. Retrieved from https://www.hbs.edu/faculty/Publication%20Files/01-002_07351ae8-58be-44e5-a6d8-205cbf5b4424.pdf, [Accessed on October 15, 2018].

Cisco (2011). *The Internet of Things How the Next Evolution of the Internet Is Changing Everything*. Retrieved from https://www.cisco.com/c/dam/en_us/about/ac79/docs/innov/IoT_IBSG_0411FINAL.pdf, [Accessed on April 2, 2018].

Cisco (2015). *Fog Computing and the Internet of Things: Extend the Cloud to Where the Things Are*. Retrieved from https://www.cisco.com/c/dam/en_us/solutions/trends/iot/docs/computing-overview.pdf, [Accessed on April 3, 2018].

Coetzee L. and Eksteen, J. (2011). The Internet of Things - promise for the future? An introduction. *2011 IST-Africa Conference Proceedings*, pp. 1–9.

Colt, S. (2014). *These 5-Speed Bumps Could Stop the Internet of Things Dead in Its Tracks*. Retrieved from http://www.businessinsider.com/internet-of-things-speed-bumps-2014-6, [Accessed on March 25, 2018].

Dahlberg, H., Öberg, J., Glaumann, M., Gjelstrup, A. and Berntsson, G.L. (2015). *Connected Things*. Arthur DeLittle TeliaSonera.

Darbee, P. (2005). *INSTEON: The Details*. In Smartphone Technology.

De Man, H. (2012). *Deliverable D3.3: Value Delivery Model and Methods, Networked Enterprise transformation and resource management in Future internet-enabled Innovation Clouds*. p. 129.

Dijkman, R.M., Sprenkels, B., Peeters, T. and Janssen, A. (2015). Business models for the Internet of Things. *International Journal of Information Management*, Vol. 35, No. 6, pp. 672–678. ISSN 0268-4012.

European Parliament's Directorate-General for Internal Policies (2015). *Over-the-Counter (OTTs) Players: Market Dynamics and Policy Challenges*. Retrieved from http://www.europarl.europa.eu/RegData/etudes/STUD/2015/569979/IPOL_STU(2015)569979_EN.pdf, [Acceded on March 27, 2017].

EY (2017). *Digital Transformation for 2020 and Beyond: A Global Telecommunications.* Study, Retrieved from https://webforms.ey. com/Publication/vwLUAssets/ey-digital-transformation-for-2020-and-beyond/$FILE/ey-digital-transformation-for-2020-and-beyond.pdf, [Accessed on March 22, 2018].

Fantana, N.L. Riedel, T., Schlick, J. and Ferber, S. (2013). Internet of Things ..., 2013 in Europe IoT Strategic Research Agenda 2012, Sergio Gusmeroli. Editor.

Fenn, J. and LeHong, H. (2011). *Hype-Cycle for Emerging Technologies 2011.* Retrieved from https://www.gartner.com/doc/1754719/hype-cycle-emerging-technologies-, [Accessed on January 10, 2019].

Frost & Sullivan (n.d.). *Mega Trends: Smart is the New Green.* Retrieved from https://ww2.frost.com/research/visionary-innovation/smart-cities-smart-new-green/, [Accessed on March 22, 2018].

Garcia-Hernando, A.-B., Martinez-Ortega, J.-F., Lopez-Navarro, J.-M., Prayati, A. and Redondo-Lopez, L. (2008). *Problem Solving for Wireless Sensor Networks.* Springer-Verlag London Limited.

Gartner (2013). *Gartner Says the Internet of Things Installed Base Will Grow to 26 Billion Units By 2020.* Retrieved from https://www.gartner.com/newsroom/id/2636073, [Accessed on March 28, 2018].

Gartner (n.d.). *I.T. Glossary. Internet of Things.* Retrieved from https://www.gartner.com/it-glossary/internet-of-things/, [Accessed on January 15, 2019].

Glova, Jozef and Sabol, Tomáš and Vajda, Viliam. (2014). Business models for the internet of things environment. *Procedia Economics and Finance,* Vol. 15 No. 1122–1129, ISSN = 2212-5671, 10.1016/S2212-5671(14)00566-8.

Gubbi, J., Buyya, R., Marusic, S. and Palaniswami, M. (2013). Internet of Things (IoT): A vision, architectural elements, and future directions. *Future Generation Computer Systems,* Vol. 29 No. 7, pp. 1645–1660.

Harald, Bauer, Patel, Mark, and Veira, Jan. (2014). *The Internet of Things: Sizing up the opportunity,* McKinsey Quarterly, December.

Helby, Z., Hartke, K., Bormann, C. and Frank, B. (2011). *Constrained Application Protocol (CoAP).* CoRE Working Group, Draft-IETF-corecoap-06.

Hoebeke, J., Carles, D., Ishaq, I., Ketema, G., Rossey, J., De Poorter, E., Moerman, I. and Demeester, P. (2012). We are Leveraging Upon Standards to Build the Internet of Things. In *Proceedings of the 19th IEEE Symposium on Communications and Vehicular Technology in the Benelux;* Eindhoven, The Netherlands.

Hui, G. (2014). How the internet of things changes business models. *Harvard Business Review.* Retrieved from https://hbr.org/2014/07/how-the-internet-of-things-changes-business-models, [Accessed on March 29].

International Telecommunication Union (ITU) (2016). *Harnessing the Internet of Things for Global Development.* Retrieved from https://www.itu.int/en/action/broadband/Documents/Harnessing-IoT-Global-Development.pdf, [Accessed March 27, 2018].

Jadeja, Y. and Modi, K. (2012). Cloud Computing – Concepts, Architecture, and Challenges. *International Conference on Computing, Electronics and Electrical Technologies (ICCEET).*

Joshi, R., Jadav, H. M., Mali, A. and Kulkarni, S. V. (2016). IoT application for a real-time monitor of PLC data using EPICS. *2016 International Conference on Internet of Things and Applications (IOTA)*, pp. 68–72. 10.1109/IOTA.2016.7562697.

Khan, R., Khan, S.U., Zaheer, R. and Khan, S. (2012). Future Internet: The Internet of Things Architecture, Possible Applications, and Key Challenges. *10th International Conference on Frontiers of Information Technology*, Islamabad, 257–260.

Kim, J. and Lee, J. (2012). Cluster-based mobility supporting WMN for IoT networks. *2012 IEEE International Conference on Green Computing and Communications*, pp. 700–703. 10.1109/GreenCom.2012.114.

Kortuem, G., Kawsar, F., Fitton, D. and Sundramoorthy, V. (2010). Smart objects as building blocks for the Internet of Things. *IEEE Internet Computing*, Vol. 14 No. 1, pp. 44–51.

Kovatsch, M., Weiss, M. and Guinard, D. (2010). Embedding Internet Technology for Home Automation. *Proceedings of ETFA*, Bilbao, Spain.

Kushalnagar, N., Montenegro, G. and Schumacher, C. (2007). I.P. v6 over Low-Power Wireless Personal Area Networks (6LoWPAN): Overview, assumptions, problem statement, and goals. Internet Engineering Task Force RFC 4919.

Lee, G.M. and Crespi, N. (2011). *The Internet of Things - Challenge for a New Architecture from Problems.* IETF Internet Architecture Board, Interconnecting Smart Objects with the Internet Workshop, Prague, Czech Republic.

Lee, G.-M. and Kim, J.-Y. (2010). The internet of things: A problem statement. *IEEE* 978-1-4244-9807-9/10.

Lovrek, I., Caric, A. and Lucic, D. (2014). Future Network and Future Internet: A Survey of Regulatory Perspective. *22nd International Conference on Software, Telecommunications, and Computer Networks (SoftCOM)*, pp. 186–191.

Mainetti, L., Patrono, L. and Vilei, A. (2011). Evolution of Wireless Sensor Networks Towards the Internet of Things: A Survey. *19th International Conference on Software, Telecommunications, and Computer Networks SoftCOM*, pp. 1–6.

Markets & Markets (IoT) Market 2017 - Global Forecast to 2022 - Research and Markets, 2017. (2017).

McKinsey Global Institute (2015). *The Internet of Things: Mapping value beyond the hype.* Retrieved from https://www.mckinsey. com/~/media/McKinsey/Business%20Functions/McKinsey%20 Digital/Our%20Insights/The%20Internet%20of%20Things%20 The%20value%20of%20digitizing%20the%20physical%20world/ The-Internet-of-things-Mapping-the-value-beyond-the-hype.ashx, [Accessed on March 26, 2018].

Meddeb, A. (2016). Internet of things standards: Who stands out from the crowd? *IEEE Communications Magazine,* Vol. 54 No. 7, pp. 40–47.

Meffert, J. and Mohr, N. (2017). *Overwhelming OTT: Telco's Growth Strategy in a Digital World.* Retrieved from https://www.mckinsey. com/industries/telecommunications/our-insights/overwhelming-ott-telcos-growth-strategy-in-a-digital-world, [Accessed March 7, 2019].

Morgan Stanley (2016). *Mighty Micro-Engines of the Internet of Things.* Retrieved from https://www.morganstanley.com/ideas/microcontrollers-semiconductors-internet-of-things, [Accessed on March 25, 2018].

Negelmann, B. (2001). Geschäftsmodell, in: Diller, H. (Hrsg.): *Vahlens Großes Marketing Lexikon,* München, Beck, p. 532.

Nick, T. (2014). *Did you Know How Many Different Kinds of Sensors go Inside a Smartphone?* Retrieved from https://www.phonearena. com/news/Did-you-know-how-many-different-kinds-of-sensors-go-inside-a-smartphone_id57885, [Accessed on March 2018].

Osterwalder, A. and Pigneur, Y. (2010). *Business Model Generation.* Hoboken, NJ, John Wiley & Sons, Inc.. ISBN: 978-0470-87641-1.

Osterwalder, A., Pigneur, Y. and Tucci, L.-C. (2004). Clarifying business models: Origins, present, and future of the concept. *Communications of AIS,* No. 16, pp. 1–25.

Palattella, M.R., Dohler, M., Grieco, A., Rizzo, G., Torsner, J., Engel, T. and Ladid, L. (2016). Internet of things in the 5G era: Enablers, architecture, and business models. *IEEE Journal on Selected Areas in Communications,* Vol. 34 No. 3, pp. 510–527.

Park, Keon Chul, Shin, D.-H. and Jin Park, Y. (2017). Understanding the Internet of Things ecosystem: Multi-level analysis of users, society, and ecology. *Digital Policy, Regulation and Governance,* Vol. 19 No. 1, pp. 77–100. 10.1108/DPRG-07-2016-0035.

Pepper, R. and Garrity, J. (2014). *The Internet of Everything: How the Network Unleashes the Benefits of Big Data.* Retrieved from http:// www3.weforum.org/docs/GITR/2014/GITR_Chapter1.2_2014. pdf, [Accessed on February 14, 2018].

Perera, C., Liu, C.H., Jayawardena, S. and Chen, M. (2015). A survey on the internet of things from an industrial market perspective. *IEEE Access,* 10.1109/ACCESS.2015.2389854.

Perera, C., Zaslavsky, A., Christen, P. and Georgakopoulos, D. (2014). I was sensing as a service model for smart cities supported by the Internet of Things. *Transactions on Emerging Telecommunications Technologies*, Vol. 25 No. 1, pp. 81–93.

PWC (2015). *Outlook Special: Over-the-Top Television.* Retrieved from https://www.pwc.nl/nl/assets/documents/pwc-outlook-special-over-the-top-television.pdf, [Accessed on March 25, 2018].

Qingjun, C. (2018). *Six IoT Models. Which should Telcos Choose?* https://www.huawei.com/ca/about-huawei/publications/communicate/84/iot-business-models-telcos

Research Above Media (2018). How IoT is changing the business world. Retrieved from https://www.reachabovemedia.com/how-iot-is-changing-the-business-world/, [Accessed December 11, 2018].

Richter, P., Allman, M., Bush, R. and Paxson, V. (2015). A primer on IPV4 scarcity. *ACM SIGCOMM Computer Communication Review* [0146-4833], Vol. 45 No. 2, pp. 21–31.

Shelby, Z. and Bormann, Carsten. (2011). *6LoWPAN. The Wireless Embedded Internet.* Wiley.

Shirvanimoghaddam, M., Dohler, M., and Johnson, S. J., Massive non-orthogonal multiple access for cellular IoT: Potentials and limitations. *IEEE Communications Magazine*, Vol. 55 No. 9, pp. 55–61. September. 10.1109/MCOM.2017.1600618.

Spencer, M.-T. and Ayoub, P.-J. (2014). Business model innovation and its impact on roles and expectations: Videon case study. *People & Strategy: The Professional Journal of HRPS*, Vol. 37 No. 1.

Teu, A. (2014). *Cloud Storage Is Eating the World Alive.* Retrieved from https://techcrunch.com/2014/08/20/cloud-storage-is-eating-alive-traditional-storage/, [Accessed on March 26, 2018].

The Economist Intelligence Unit (2013). *The Internet of Things Business Index: A Quiet Revolution Gathers Pace.* Retrieved from https://www.arm.com/files/pdf/EIU_Internet_Business_Index_WEB. PDF, [Accessed on March 26, 2018].

The Economist Intelligence Unit (2017). *The Internet of Things Business Index 2017: Transformation in Motion.* Retrieved from https://www.eiuperspectives.economist.com/sites/default/files/EIU-ARM-IBM%20IoT%20Business%20Index%202017%20copy.pdf, [Accessed on March 26, 2018].

Timmers, P. (1998). Business models for electronic markets. *Journal on Electronic Markets*, Vol. 8 No. 2, pp. 3–8.

Turber, S. and Smiela, C. (2014). A Business Model Type for the Internet of Things. *22nd European Conference on Information Systems (ECIS 2014)*, At Tel Aviv, Israel.

Vermesan, O. and Friess, P. (2011). *Internet of Things – Global Technological and Societal Trends.* River Publishers. ISBN 978-87-92329-67-7.

Vermesan, O. and Friess, P. (2013). *Internet of Things: Covering Technologies for Intelligent Environments and Integrated Ecosystems.* River Publishers Series in Communications.

Vermesan, O. et al. (2011). Internet of Things Strategic Research Agenda. *Chapter 2 in the Internet of Things—Global Technological and Societal Trends,* River Publishers. ISBN 978-87-92329-67-7.

Vermesan, O., Friess, P., Guillemin, P., Sundmaeker, H., Eisenhauer, M. and Moessner Baldini, G. (2014). Internet of Things and Innovation Agenda. [Chapter 3]. In Vermesan, O. and Friess, P. (Eds.). *Internet of Things – From Research and Innovation to Market Deployment,* River Publishers.

Vineela, S. and Meze, A. (2015). Evolution of wireless sensor networks towards the internet of things. *International Journal of Eminent Engineering Technologies,* Vol. 3 No. 4.

West, D.M. (2016). How 5G technology enables the health internet of things. *Center for Technology Innovation at Brookings.* Retrieved from https://www.brookings.edu/wp-content/uploads/2016/07/5G-Health-Internet-of-Things_West.pdf, [Accessed on April 1, 2018].

Westerlund, W. (Mika), Leminen, Seppo and Rajahonka, Mervi. (2014). Designing business models for the Internet of Things. *Technology Innovation Management Review,* pp. 5–14, 2014-07-01.

Yüksel, I. (2012). Developing a multi-criteria decision-making model for PESTEL analysis. *International Journal of Business and Management,* Vol. 7, pp. 52–66.

Zanella, A., Bui, N., Castellani, A., Vangelista, L. and Zorzi, M. (2014). Internet of things for smart cities. *IEEE Internet of Things Journal,* Vol. 1 No. 1, pp. 22–32.

ZigBee Alliance (2007). *ZigBee Home Automation Public Application Profile.* Revision 25, v. 1.0, Oct. 2007.

Z-Wave (2007). *Z-Wave Protocol Overview.* Version 4.

ADDITIONNAL REFERENCES

Andersson, P. and Mattsson, L.G. (2015). Service innovations enabled by the internet of things. *IMP Journal,* Vol. 9 No. 1, pp. 85–106.

Arthur, A.L. (2018). A maturing Internet of Things: Realizing the next level of value. Sourced

Buttarelli, G. (2010). Internet of Things: Ubiquitous Monitoring in Space and Time, *European Privacy and Data Protection Commissioners' Conference,* Prague, April 29.

Claudy, M.C., Garcia, R. and O'Driscoll, A. (2015). Consumer resistance to innovation—a behavioral reasoning perspective. *Journal of the Academy of Marketing Science,* Vol. 43 No. 4, pp. 528–544.

Dutton, W.H. (2014). Putting things to work: Social and policy challenges for the internet of things. *Info,* Vol. 16 No. 3, pp. 1–21.

European Commission (2013). Report on the consultation on IoT governance, European Commission, Brussels, January 16. Retrieved from http://www.adlittle.com/

Haghi, M., Thurow, K. and Stoll, R. (2017). Wearable devices in medical internet of things: Scientific research and commercially available devices. *Healthcare Informatics Research*, Vol. 23 No. 1, pp. 4–15.

Kang, Y., Han, M., Han, K. and Kim, J. (2015). A study of internet of things applications. *Advanced Science and Technology Letters*, Vol. 107, pp. 1–4.

Kingsley, A.F., van den Bergh, R.G. and Bonardi, J.-P. (2012). Political markets and regulatory uncertainty: Insights and implications for integrated strategy. *Academy of Management Perspectives*, Vol. 26 No. 3, pp. 52–67.

Mani, Z. and Chouk, I. (2017). Drivers of consumers' resistance to smart products. *Journal of Marketing Management*, Vol. 33 Nos 1–2, pp. 76–97.

Miller, F.P., Vandome, A.F. and McBrewster, J. (2011). *Pest Analysis*, VDM Publishing.

Oh, L.B. and Teo, H.H. (2010). Consumer value co-creation in a hybrid commerce service-delivery system. *International Journal of Electronic Commerce*, Vol. 14 No. 3, pp. 35–62.

Porter, M. (2014). How smart, connected products are transforming competition. *Harvard Business Review*, November, Vol. 92 No. 11, pp. 4–23.

Shin, D. (2014). A socio-technical framework for internet-of-things design. *Telematics and Informatics*, Vol. 31 No. 4, pp. 519–531.

Shin, D. and Park, Y. (2017). Understanding the internet of things ecosystem: A multi-level analysis of users, society, and ecology. *Digital Policy, Regulation and Governance*, Vol. 19 No. 1, pp. 77–100.

The Economist Intelligence Unit (2018). THE INTERNET THINGS BUSINESS INDEX: A quiet revolution gathers pace, United Nations Report (2015), "World population aging," Department of Economic and Social Affairs Population Division, New York, NY, Retrieved from www.un.org/en/development/desa/population/publications/pdf/ageing/WPA2015_Report.pdf

Trequattrini, R., Shams, R., Lardo, A. and Lombardi, R. (2016). Risk of an epidemic impact when adopting the internet of things: The role of sector-based resistance. *Business Process Management Journal*, Vol. 22 No. 2, pp. 403–419.

Weber, R.H. (2010). Internet of things: New security and privacy challenges. *Computer Law & Security Review*, Vol. 26 No. 1, pp. 23–30.

Weber, R.H. (2013). Internet of things – Governance quo vadis? *Computer Law & Security Review*, Vol. 29 No. 4, pp. 341–347.

INDEX

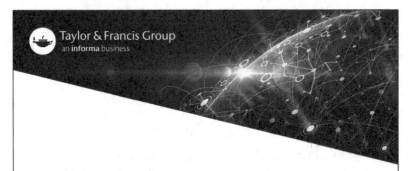